WAR AT SEA
IN THE
AGE OF SAIL
1650–1850

WAR AT SEA
IN THE
AGE OF SAIL
1650–1850

ANDREW LAMBERT

General Editor: John Keegan

CASSELL

This book is dedicated to my students.
It is only through teaching that one can truly learn.

Cassell, Wellington House, 125 Strand, London WC2R 0BB
www.cassell.co.uk

First published in Great Britain, 2000
This paperback edition 2002

British Library Cataloguing-in-publication Data
ISBN: 0-304-36351-0

Cartography: Arcadia Editions Ltd
Designer: Richard Carr
Printed and bound in Spain

Title Page: *The attempted destruction of the* Andrew *by a Dutch fireship at the battle
of Scheveningen, 31 July 1653. The ship was badly damaged, the admiral and many of
the crew were killed, but she was saved when other ships came to her assistance. The
Dutch lacked the firepower to deal with the bigger English battleships, so fireships
were their only opportunity to even the balance. (Van de Velde the Younger)*

Overleaf: *Nelson lies mortally wounded on the upper deck of HMS* Victory.
(J. M. Turner)

Acknowledgements

I HAVE THREE MAJOR debts to acknowledge at the beginning of this book. The first is to John Keegan, who invited me to write for his series, and made the offer irresistible by assembling such a strong team of authors, supported by a fine publisher. The second is to all those historians who have contributed to the development of our understanding of the naval aspects of the past. Without them there would have been little to say. While I have noted the major texts in the guide to further reading, this can only give a sample of the range and quality of modern scholarship. The final debt is to my students. My understanding of the naval past has been challenged by the need to teach an impressive body of undergraduate and postgraduate students in the unique environment of the Department of War Studies at King's College, London. Their interest, and the high quality of there questions, have forced me to reconsider the subject and the issues afresh year after year. Their input has been, and continues to be, invaluable. Although this book may lack a little of the polemical vigour of a seminar, I hope it too will stimulate further enquiry.

During the writing of the book I have acquired fresh debts, which this page can only provide an inadequate opportunity to acknowledge. The initial phase of writing the text tested the patience of my family, and I must thank Zohra, Tama-Sophie and my parents for their support. The team at Cassell, and most especially Penny Gardiner, have made the process of transforming a text into a book a pleasure, and along with Malcolm Swanston they are responsible for the quality of presentation, illustration and integration. All else rests on my head.

ANDREW LAMBERT
Kew

Contents

Acknowledgements   5
Map list   9
Chronology   10

INTRODUCTION: WAR AND INDUSTRIALIZATION   20

1 THE ORGANIZATION OF NAVIES   28

2 THE ANGLO-DUTCH WARS AND THE
   ORIGINS OF MODERN NAVAL POWER 1650–74   56

3 THE RISE AND FALL OF THE FRENCH NAVY 1680–1713   78

4 THE BALTIC IN THE EIGHTEENTH CENTURY:
   SEAPOWER IN AN INLAND SEA   94

5 THE DAWN OF GLOBAL CONFLICT 1739–63   104

6 REVERSE AND RECOVERY:
   BRITAIN VERSUS THE WORLD 1776–82   128

7 TOTAL WAR: BRITAIN, FRANCE AND THE
   STRUGGLE FOR SURVIVAL 1793–1802   150

8 SEAPOWER AND LANDPOWER:
   THE NAPOLEONIC WARS 1803–15   172

9 THE WAR OF 1812   192

10 PAX BRITANNICA? THE LAST YEARS OF SEAPOWER
   UNDER SAIL 1815–50   208

Battlefleet tonnages   218
Biographies   220
Further reading   227
Index   230
Picture credits   240

KEY TO MAPS

Military movements

→ attack

⇢ retreat

✕ battle

Geographical symbols

⬟ urban area

—— road

—— river

- - - seasonal river

····· canal

—— border

side view British ship

view from above

ship on fire/damaged

side view French ship

view from above

ship on fire/damaged

Map list

1. THE MEDITERRANEAN AND THE BLACK SEA 1651–1840   32–3

2. THE CHANNEL, NORTH SEA AND DANISH NARROWS *c.* 1800   62

3. BATTLE OF GABBARD SHOAL, 2–3 JUNE 1653   64–5

4. THE FOUR DAYS BATTLE, 1–4 JUNE 1666   70–72

5. BATTLES IN THE BALTIC   97

6. SECOND BATTLE OF SVENSKSUND, 9–10 JULY 1790   102

7. IMPERIAL AGE EMPIRES *c.* 1760   108–9

8. BATTLE OF QUIBERON BAY, 20 NOVEMBER 1759   122–3

9. BATTLE OF CHESAPEAKE BAY, 5 SEPTEMBER 1781
   THE CAMPAIGN FOR YORKTOWN: THE STRATEGIC VIEW   140–41

10. BATTLE OF THE SAINTES, 12 APRIL 1782   142–3

11. BATTLE OF THE GLORIOUS FIRST OF JUNE, PHASES 1 AND 2   158

12. BATTLE OF THE NILE, ABOUKIR BAY, 1–2 AUGUST 1798   162–3

13. BATTLE OF TRAFALGAR, 21 OCTOBER 1805   180–81

14. BRITISH NEW ORLEANS CAMPAIGN,
    22 NOVEMBER 1814 – 11 FEBRUARY 1815;   194
    THE GREAT LAKES AND US EASTERN SEABOARD   195

15. *SHANNON–CHESAPEAKE* ACTION, 1 JUNE 1813   200–201

16. ACRE, 3 NOVEMBER 1840   214

Chronology

1652–4	**First Anglo-Dutch War.**
19 May 1652	Battle of Dover.
26 Aug 1652	Battle of Plymouth.
28 Sept 1652	Battle of Kentish Knock: Blake defeats Witte de With.
30 Nov 1652	Battle of Dungeness: Tromp defeats Blake.
28 Feb –	Battle of Portland: first use of linear tactics by English:
2 March 1653	Blake defeats Tromp.
2–3 June 1653	Battle of Gabbard Shoal: Monck defeats Tromp.
31 July 1653	Battle of Scheveningen: Tromp killed, but Dutch break English blockade, despite heavy losses.
5 Apr 1654	Treaty of Westminster: English secure Navigation Acts and St Helena.
1656–9	**Anglo-Spanish War.**
(1655)	Jamaica captured by Admiral Penn.
1656	Blake captures part of the silver flota off Cádiz.
20 Apr 1657	Battle of Santa Cruz: Blake destroy silver flota at Tenerife.
1665–7	**Second Anglo-Dutch War:** English begin war with attacks on Dutch African possessions and convoys.
3 June 1665	Battle of Lowestoft: James, Duke of York defeats Opdam.
1–4 June 1666	Four Days battle. Monck and Rupert divided, Monck heavily engaged by de Ruyter, tactical victory for Dutch.
4–5 Aug 1666	St James's Day battle: Monck and Rupert reverse the verdict of the previous battle, regaining command of the Channel.
19–23 June 1667	De Ruyter sails into the Medway and captures part of the English fleet, which has been paid off as an economy measure.
21 July 1667	Treaty of Breda: England secures New York.
1672–4	**Third Anglo-Dutch War.**
1672–80	**Franco-Dutch War.**
March 1672	English attack Dutch channel convoy.

28 May 1672	Battle of Sole Bay: de Ruyter attacks allied fleet under James, Duke of York, pre-empting an invasion of Holland.
July 1672	Allied fleet in the Texel: landing prevented by presence of Dutch fleet.
28 May 1673	First battle of Schooneveld: Rupert and de Ruyter, inconclusive.
14 June 1673	Second battle of Schooneveld: de Ruyter again frustrates invasion.
21 Aug 1673	Battle of the Texel: inconclusive battle noted for the refusal of the French, under d'Estrees, to engage closely.
Feb 1674	Second Treaty of Westminster: English peace with Dutch.
22 Apr 1676	Battle of Augusta: Duquense and de Ruyter, inconclusive; de Ruyter mortally wounded.
2 June 1676	Battle of Palermo: French fireships destroy Dutch and Spanish fleets.
1688–97	**War of the League of Augsburg.**
Nov 1688	Dutch fleet lands William of Orange and his army at Torbay.
1 May 1689	Battle of Bantry Bay: inconclusive; Londonderry later relieved.
30 June 1690	Battle of Beachy Head: Tourville defeats Anglo-Dutch under Torrington, ten ships lost. French have command of the Channel, but do nothing.
1691	Tourville cruises against trade.
1692	Louis XIV plans an invasion of England: 30,000 men collected in Normandy, to restore James II.
29 May – 3 June 1692	Battle of Barfleur: Tourville, although far weaker, ordered to engage, and fights the allied fleet to a standstill.
22 May 1692	Fifteen French ships, mostly three-deckers, are destroyed by English fireships off Cherbourg and La Hougue. French fleet no longer capable of competing with the allies, despite large number of ships, due to shortage of men, guns and stores.

27–28 June 1693	Tourville captures a large part of the Smyrna convoy from Rooke.
20 Sept – 30 Oct 1697	Peace conference for Treaty of Ryswick.
1697	Father Paul Hoste, Tourville's secretary and chaplain, publishes the first theoretical work on fleet tactics.
1701–14	**War of the Spanish Succession.**
29 Aug – 3 Sept 02	Action off Cartagena, Benbow's attack on French squadron beaten off due to the cowardice of four of his captains; two executed.
12 Oct 1702	Attack on Vigo: Rooke captures Spanish treasure fleet and French escort in harbour.
24 July 1704	Rooke captures Gibraltar.
13 Aug 1704	Battle of Malaga: indecisive action, but Rooke blocks Toulouse's attempt to recapture Gibraltar. Only fleet action of the war.
July–Aug 1707	Eugene and Shovell make a combined attack on Toulon: French fleet scuttled, but city held.
7 June 1708	English destroy a Spanish silver fleet off Cartagena.
1708	Minorca taken by British.
Sept 1712	Duguay-Trouin captures and ransoms Rio de Janeiro.
1713	Treaty of Utrecht.
1714	Rastatt and Baden.
1700–1721	**Great Northern War.**
6 Aug 1714	Battle off Hango: 100 Russian galleys capture seven Swedish sailing ships after a day-long battle. Russian losses high.
1718–20	**War for Sicily.**
11 Aug 1718	Battle of Cape Passaro: George Byng destroys Spanish fleet under Casteneta in a dynamic pursuit action.
1740–48	**War of the Austrian Succession.**
1739	Capture of Porto Bello by Vernon.

1740	Vernon's attack on Cartagena fails due to poor inter-service co-ordination, and disease.
11 Feb 1744	Battle of Toulon: inconclusive action between Franco-Spanish fleet and British under Matthews, who is cashiered for failing to press the battle.
1745	Capture of Louisbourg.
25 July 1746	Battle of Negapatam: la Bourdonnais defeats British under Peyton, leading to loss of Madras.
3 May 1747	First battle of Finisterre: Anson captures French convoy escort one third his strength in pursuit battle.
14 Oct 1747	Second Battle of Finisterre: Hawke captures most of a French convoy escort two thirds his strength. French have no more squadrons left.
1748	Treaty of Aix-la-Chapelle.
1756–63	**The Seven Years War.**
10 June 1755	Boscawen's partial interception of de la Motte off Louisbourg.
20 May 1756	Battle of Minorca: John Byng and la Galissonière fight an inconclusive battle, but Minorca falls to French as a result.
14 Mar 1757	Byng court martialled and shot *'pour encourager les autres'*.
1758	Boscawen captures Louisbourg; six French battleships taken.
1759	Quebec taken by Wolfe and Admiral Saunders.
18–19 Aug 1759	Battle off Lagos: Boscawen takes or destroys five of de la Clue's seven ships, preventing him joining Brest fleet for projected invasion.
10 Sept 1759	Battle of Porto Novo (India): indecisive clash between Pocock and d'Ache, but d'Ache has no local base at which to repair, and so hands command of the sea to Pocock.
20 Nov 1759	Battle of Quiberon Bay: Hawke routs Conflans and destroys the Brest fleet in a dramatic inshore pursuit. One of the greatest naval victories.
8 June 1761	British capture Belle-Île off French coast as a blockade base.

June–Aug 1762	Havana taken by Pocock and Albermarle; nine battleships taken.
1762	Manila taken.
1763	Peace of Paris.
1768–74	**First Russo-Turkish War.**
5 July 1770	Battle of Chios. Turks driven into Chesmé Bay.
6–7 July 1770	Battle of Chesmé: Turks destroyed by fireships.
1775–83	**War of American Independence.**
27 July 1778	Battle of Ushant: Keppel and d'Orvilliers exchange fire in the Channel.
6 July 1779	Battle of Grenada: Byron and d'Estaing; inconclusive, but French capture the island.
16 Jan 1780	Battle of Cape St Vincent, or 'Moonlight battle': Rodney destroys Langara's Spanish squadron while escorting relief convoy to Gibraltar.
1780	League of the Armed Neutrality.
17 Apr 1780	Battle of Martinique: Rodney outmanoeuvres de Guichen, but failure to explain his tactics to his subordinates ruins his plan. Inconclusive action.
5 Aug 1781	Battle of the Dogger Bank: Parker and Zoutman fight to a standstill while their convoys proceed unmolested.
5 Sept 1781	Battle of Chesapeake Bay: de Grasse prevents Graves from relieving Cornwallis's army, leading to capitulation of Yorktown.
25–26 Jan 1782	Battle of St Kitts: Hood outmanoeuvres de Grasse, but as island falls Hood withdraws to link up with Rodney.
11 Apr 1782	Battle of Provindien: one of a series of indecisive engagements between the skilled tactician Suffren, and the better-manned ships under the resolute Hughes.

12 Apr 1782	Battle of the Saintes: Rodney exploits a shift in the wind to destroy cohesion of French line; de Grasse and seven ships taken. The decisive battle of the war.
Sept 1782	Great attack on Gibraltar: floating batteries destroyed.
Oct 1782	Howe relieves Gibraltar.
1783	Peace of Versailles.
1788–90	**Russo-Swedish War.**
3 July 1790	Swedish breakout from Viborg; successful withdrawal of blockaded fleet.
9–10 July 1790	Second battle of Svensksund: Russian attack on Swedish fleet repulsed; counter-attack and rough weather leads to a rout of the Russians.
14 Aug 1790	Peace of Verela.
1793–1802	**French Revolutionary Wars.**
Feb 1793	Britain joins the war.
Aug–Dec 1793	Allied occupation of Toulon: part of French fleet destroyed.
28 May – 1 June 1794	Glorious First of June: Howe decisively defeats Villaret-Joyeuse in the fleet action (seven taken), but the grain convoy to France, the object of the French sortie, escapes.
Jan 1795	French Brest fleet loses five ships in a storm.
14 Mar 1795	Battle off Genoa: Hotham takes two ships from French under Martin, preventing an attack on Corsica.
17 June 1795	Action off Belle-Île: Cornwallis with five ships escapes from Villaret-Joyeuse's twelve by skilful tactical retreat and *ruse de guerre*.
23 June 1795	Battle off Île de Groix: Bridport defeats Villaret-Joyeuse, taking three of his twelve ships.
13 July 1795	Action off Hyeres: Hotham defeats Martin; one French ship burnt.
1796	French invasion of Ireland, largely defeated by weather.

14 Feb 1797	Battle of Cape St Vincent: Jervis, with the aid of Nelson's initiative, decisively defeats de Cordova's far larger fleet; four taken.
Apr–Aug 1797	Royal Navy mutinies at Spithead and Nore.
24/5 July 1797	Nelson defeated at Tenerife; loses arm.
11 Oct 1797	Battle of Camperdown: Duncan's dynamic attack in columns defeats de Winter's Dutch fleet, after a stubborn action.
1–2 May 1798	Battle of the Nile: Nelson annihilates Brueys's fleet; only two from thirteen escape. Bonaparte's Egyptian army trapped.
Aug 1799	British landing in Holland: capture of the last Dutch battleships at Den Helder.
Feb–Mar 1801	New Armed Neutrality.
2 Apr 1801	Battle of Copenhagen: Nelson forces Danes out of Armed Neutrality after costly assault on fleet and floating defences.
6 July 1801	Battle of Algeciras: Linois beats off Saumarez, and takes one battleship.
12 July 1801	Action off Cádiz: Saumarez defeats Linois at sea; three allied ships lost.
15 Aug 1801	Nelson attacks Boulogne flotilla; beaten off with heavy losses.
March 1802	Peace of Amiens.
1803–5	Napoleon prepares for an invasion of Britain.
1803–15	**Napoleonic Wars.**
1805	Villeneuve escapes from Toulon; Nelson pursues him to West Indies. Cornwallis holds Ganteaume inside Brest.
22 June 1805	Battle of Finisterre: Calder defeats Villeneuve and forces him back to Spain.
21 Oct 1805	Battle of Trafalgar. Nelson destroys Villeneuve's larger allied fleet with a dynamic attack in two columns; eighteen taken or destroyed. Nelson killed.

4 Nov 1805	Battle of Cape Ortegal: Dumanoir with four fleeing from Trafalgar captured by Strachan.
Jan 1806	Cape Town captured by Popham.
6 Feb 1806	Battle of San Domingo: Duckworth destroys Lessigues's squadron of six battleships.
2 Oct 1806	Boulogne set ablaze by Congreve rockets fired by British boats.
Feb 1807	Duckworth passes up the Dardanelles, but Turks reject his demands and he retires with loss.
2–4 Sept 1807	Bombardment of Copenhagen: amphibious force under Cathcart and Gambier make Danes surrender their fleet, to stop it falling into French hands. Masterpiece of amphibious power projection. Results in a 'gunboat war' between Britain and the Danes in the Baltic Approaches, 1807–14, that threatens British trade routes.
Nov 1807	Portuguese fleet and royal family evacuated from Lisbon to Brazil.
Sept 1808	Russian Mediterranean fleet blockaded at Lisbon and crews sent home.
10–11 Apr 1809	Battle of the Aix Roads: Gambier traps Willaumez, but does not support Captain Lord Cochrane's astonishing explosion vessel, fire-ship and rocket attack.
Aug 1809	Walcheren Expedition: Strachan and Chatham fail to impose any haste on the 40,000-man expedition to destroy Antwerp, so results are disappointing, and losses to disease high.
26 Oct and 31 Oct 1809	Actions off Cette and Rosas: French fleet sent to reinforce Barcelona destroyed by British.
13 Mar 1811	Battle of Lissa: Hoste destroys a Franco-Venetian frigate squadron to secure command of the Adriatic.
1812–15	**War of 1812.**
19 Aug 1812	USS *Constitution* captures HMS *Guerriere*.
25 Oct 1812	USS *United States* takes HMS *Macedonian*.

On 1 June 1813 HMS Shannon, *under Captain Philip Broke, engaged the USS*
Chesapeake *off Boston, in a single-ship action of unparalled intensity. Broke, seen
here in the mêlée on* Chesapeake's *upper deck, survived despite appalling injuries.
The carnage around the action reflects the ferocity of this engagement: more than
one third of those involved became casualties.*

29 Nov 1812	USS *Constitution* takes HMS *Java*.
Mar 1813	British under Cockburn ravage Chesapeake Bay region.
1 June 1813	HMS *Shannon* captures USS *Chesapeake*, perhaps the most brilliant single-ship action in the age of sailing warships.
28 Mar 1814	HMS *Phoebe* captures the USS *Essex*, relying on long-range gunnery.
24–5 Aug 1814	Capture of Washington by amphibious force under Ross and Cockburn. Ascent of Potomac by British frigates.
12–14 Sept 1814	Attack on Baltimore.
24 Dec 1814	Treaty of Ghent.
8 Jan 1815	Battle of New Orleans.
15 Jan 1815	Capture of USS *President*.
1815	Treaty of Vienna.

1816	The British bombard Algiers to end Christian slavery.
1816	American squadrons force North African states to abandon piracy.
1816–27	**Latin and South American Wars of Independence:** British mercenary involvement, notably Lord Cochrane in Chile, Peru and Brazil.
1822	British river operations in Burma.
1822–7	**Greek War of Independence.**
20 Oct 1827	Battle of Navarino: British, French and Russian fleet under Codrington destroys Turko-Egyptian squadron. Greece independent.
1833–5	**Portuguese Civil War.**
5 July 1833	Battle of Cape St Vincent: Captain Charles Napier RN changes course of Portuguese war while serving as a mercenary.
1834–40	**Carlist War in Spain:** British forces active on Spanish coast.
1838	**French-Mexican War:** Vera Cruz bombarded.
1840	**Syrian campaign:** British fleet drives Egyptian army out of Palestine by interdicting seaborne supplies and then capturing isolated fortresses. Restores Turkish rule over Egypt, and deters France.
3 Nov 1840	Bombardment and capture of Acre by a sailing battlefleet with a handful of steamships in attendance.
1846–8	**Mexican-American War:** Large-scale amphibious power projection. Conquest of California.
9 Mar 1847	American amphibious landing at Vera Cruz, leading to capture of Mexico City and end of war.
1848	**Prusso-Danish War.**
1851	Completion of the French 90-gun steam battleship *Le Napoléon*, the first purpose-built steam battleship, marks the end of the age of sail.
1855	The first all-steam fleet, the British Baltic Fleet, goes to war.

War and Industrialization

In the first years of the seventeenth century galleys were still used as front-line warships, particularly for inshore and amphibious operations, as seen in this detail from Willaerts's painting showing a Dutch attack on a Spanish fortress in the Low Countries, dated 1622. (Adam Willaerts)

War and Industrialization

ALTHOUGH THE FASCINATION with the drama of war at sea in the age of sail is as strong as it has ever been, and despite a literary genre which supplements existing accounts, the subject has become isolated from the wider historical consciousness by the passage of time and by the revolution in maritime technology. As a result, the context in which naval operations occur is rarely drawn with sufficient breadth to make the movement of ships and fleets anything more than an excuse for discussing battle. It is only by addressing the political, diplomatic, strategic, social, economic and scientific contexts within which navies operate, that war at sea becomes an intelligible field of study. Before examining the conduct of war it is necessary to address the themes that will be developed in this book: the nature of seapower, the shape of navies, ship design, bases, guns and tactics. Thereafter, the narrative chapters will consider why navies were built, linking them to national policy, commercial activity and imperial ambition, examining how they were used and how they developed.

SEAPOWER

The strategic value of maritime strength, commonly called 'seapower', has been a major factor in the history of war. Seapower is created and used as an instrument of state policy. Throughout history, nations have chosen to acquire and use this instrument in various shapes and forms, their choices governed by the importance of the sea to the individual nation as a defensive necessity or an offensive opportunity. The exact form that national navies have taken reflects the depth of the individual state's financial commitment, often determined by the primacy of other demands like the army, the availability of suitable officers and men, the state of contemporary technology and, ultimately, the degree to which seapower is critical to the survival of the state. Here there is a distinction between maritime powers, those who depend on the sea for their very survival, and naval powers, those that have no vital interests at sea, and use their naval strength to advance national power. While this distinction is theoretical, and most nations fall between the two extremes, it is important to recognize that the navy built by a maritime trading empire will be quite different from that of a land-based power with continental ambitions. The very different histories of the British Royal Navy and the Russian Imperial Navy in this period reflect that fact.

By 1650 European states had established a monopoly over the use of violence at sea, stamping out piracy in their own waters. Further afield, the situation was less satisfactory, with the North African pirate states and Caribbean piracy only suppressed in the 1830s. In the South China Sea the pirates survived into the steam age. State control of violence at sea was the key to the taxation of maritime trade. It also allowed states to license private contractors, or 'privateers', to attack enemy merchant shipping for profit. Privateers were a useful supplement to national naval power when the regular forces were weak, but added little to the profile of a dominant navy.

Seapower does not work like military power. For all the fascination they exert the large, apparently 'decisive', naval battles of this period were in fact peculiarly indecisive. As the great maritime strategist Sir Julian Corbett once observed, the immediate results of Trafalgar were singularly small. By contrast, in 1806 Napoleon's victory at the battle of Jena led to the overthrow of the Prussian state. Seapower could not overthrow a major European state. Seapower is attritional, with battles and campaigns forming part of the gradual, cumulative process that wears down an enemy's resources and creates a dominant position at sea that can be turned to strategic advantage. At heart this is an economic question. After Trafalgar Britain used her seapower to isolate Napoleon in Europe, controlling access to the rest of the world to bolster her economy and engage France in a long war of economic attrition. Unable to engage the British at sea, Napoleon launched a counter-blockade, the 'Continental System', intended to exclude Britain from Europe. Ultimately, he launched two military campaigns, in Spain and Russia, to force these countries to join the Continental

System, which eventually brought down his empire. Although the military power that defeated Napoleon was largely provided by European armies, it was British maritime power that provided them with the money and weapons to fight, while her army kept open the Iberian theatre and her diplomacy built the final coalition.

The basic instrument of economic attrition and political coercion applied by seapower was the blockade. By 1650 warships were capable of maintaining station off a hostile coast for long enough to deny those being blockaded access to the sea. A commercial blockade, intended to cut the economic lifeline of the state, was a powerful weapon against a maritime nation, particularly one that depended on the sea for food. Against continental empires it took far longer to bite. Military blockades denied the enemy navy opportunities to go to sea, and were usually aimed at preventing the movement of troops for invasion. The two types of blockade have often been confused under a single heading, but their requirements were quite distinct. The former necessarily relied

on dispersed fleets, mainly comprising cruisers, to watch every small harbour; the latter required battle fleets to watch the main enemy bases. The ability to impose either type of blockade developed significantly over the period 1650–1850, and was one of the key elements in the increasing strategic significance of seapower.

Since the dawn of organized warfare the fundamental importance of the sea has been the degree to which seapower can influence events on land, and it is there that the real value of naval power lies. The strategic impact of maritime power on the land takes many forms, from the most obvious – the bombardment of coastal towns, the amphibious power to land and sustain troops and the seizure of overseas territories – to economic warfare, the capture of ships, the closure of sea routes and blockade. Consequently, almost every naval battle can be directly related to events on land.

The human race lives on land and many of the basic dynamics of military operations do not apply at sea. Possession, in the simplest

Commodore Nelson, on board HMS Theseus, *commanding the inshore squadron blockading Cádiz, July 1797. A close blockade prevented the enemy fleet, seen in the distance, from leaving harbour, and also denied them food and shipbuilding stores. This could force the enemy to dismantle their ships and pay off their crew. (Thomas Butterworth)*

terms, is of little value. However, the seas have always been harvested, taxed and exploited. Naval warfare has expanded and developed in harmony with the increasing value of maritime resources and communications. Important waterways have been controlled and taxed by local powers – the Danish imposition of 'Sound Dues' on merchant ships passing the Baltic narrows is a classic example. Similarly, the English demanded a salute to their claim of 'Sovereignty of the Sea' over the Channel, a claim they upheld by gunfire, and used as a pretext for at least one war. Fishing in territorial waters, usually up to three miles from shore, could be taxed. Long-distance trade provided profits and customs revenues, while colonial conquests enhanced the value of trade by controlling access to markets and raw materials. All maritime trades could be 'harvested' of seamen to crew warships by impressment.

The basis of any sustained maritime power was oceanic trade. It was on the results of long-distance commerce, here with the East Indies, that Holland created her naval strength. That strength was required to escort the merchant ships, whose taxes paid for the war fleet. (H. C. Vroom)

DETERRENCE

Because navies have always been expensive to use, and take time to produce results, they have often been employed to deter war. By mobilizing or threatening to use naval power nations can often secure their aims without war. The British were active, and generally effective, exponents of deterrence after 1763. As part of a carefully calculated diplomatic position, a naval demonstration could be very effective. Similarly, naval arms races were used as an alternative to war. Maritime powers such as Holland and Britain were forced to respond when 'continental' rivals like France increased their naval strength, in order to preserve their diplomatic freedom of action. In an arms race the political commitment of the state, the depth of the public purse and the strength of the maritime industrial base were the key elements. Arms races were attractive options for maritime economies, as they avoided the dislocation and losses of a real war. They stressed that the key to victory lay in the totality of national resources: the naval, mercantile, political, human and industrial assets that make up maritime power. They gave maritime powers, which had large, transferable maritime resource bases, a massive advantage over purely naval powers, in which the private sector could not provide the shipbuilding facilities and seafaring labour required to accelerate their effort.

Between 1650 and 1850 the strategic significance of seapower developed exponentially. From a limited instrument, capable of seasonal operations in the narrow seas around Europe, sailing navies developed into wide-ranging units of almost unlimited endurance. In the interval navies had created and destroyed colonial empires, changed the European balance of power, crushed the last remnants of non-European power and established something close to a global empire. All this was achieved without fundamental changes in the instruments of war at sea. Before turning to consider how these momentous changes were brought about, it is necessary to examine the basis of naval power, a process made easier by the relative stability of ships and systems, manpower and the operational art.

CHAPTER ONE

The Organization of Navies

The French dockyard at Brest in 1794. Brest, the main French base throughout this period, was ideally placed for Atlantic warfare, and sufficiently far from the sea to be secure from all but the largest amphibious assault. The French fleet sortied from Brest in 1794 to cover an inbound grain convoy, leading to the battle of the Glorious First of June. (Jean-François Hue)

The Organization of Navies

Between 1650 and 1850 navies developed from small forces, largely reinforced with hired merchant ships in wartime, to vast bureaucratic standing services which imposed professional standards on officers and, increasingly, on men, and had large reserves of purpose-built warships, dockyards and arsenals devoted to their maintenance. Each state developed its own style of naval administration, but the basic requirement of sustained political and financial support, with informed political decision-making, was actually achieved by surprisingly few – essentially only the maritime powers.

Navies developed alongside the nation states that they served. Only strong, centrally controlled states had the tax-raising powers to fund standing navies, which, like contemporary armies, were invariably involved in revenue collection. Within those states, support for navies came from a variety of sources. In absolutist regimes the personal wishes of the monarch prevailed. Often prestige was more important than fighting strength, although the two requirements were not necessarily mutually exclusive. Republics and constitutional monarchies proved better able to sustain naval power, for the politics of such states reflected the interests of several groups that benefited from naval strength: merchants, coastal towns, colonial speculators and investors. That these states also tended to be maritime indicates a strong link between the economic life of the nation and the political system it develops. Through the power of the purse, these groups determined what type of navy was maintained, and often how it was used.

Each state built a navy to meet its individual needs. A close examination of the mixture of ship types, officers and men, infrastructure and administration that the major nations acquired is the most compelling evidence of their aims and ambitions. States with extensive maritime interests would try to control the seas for their own use, and to deny them to their rivals. The classic sea-control

Without a powerful industrial base navies could not function. In the eighteenth century battleship anchors were among the largest iron forgings manufactured, and demanded a large investment in plant and skilled labour. Given the fundamental importance of the anchor, the work had to be of high quality. The anchor being worked on here is a single fluke mooring anchor.

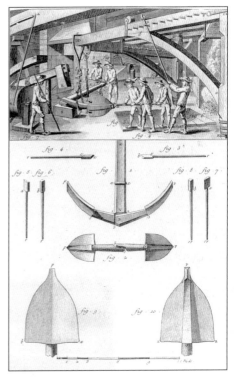

strategy of the sailing ship era required a superior battle fleet to secure command, either by defeating the enemy fleet in battle, or by blockading it in its base. When control of the sea was in doubt, navies could attempt to exert local or temporary sea control for specific purposes, such as escorting merchant ships. Spain and, after 1714, the Netherlands built cruiser navies to convoy their merchant shipping, because they depended on sea communications but lacked the economic power to achieve sea control. A state without vital maritime interests could resort to sea denial, attempting to limit the ability of the dominant navy to exploit the sea. This was usually accomplished by attacking merchant shipping, the French *guerre de course* (literally a 'war of the chase'), destroying commerce with naval vessels and privateers. The French also used their fleet for colonial operations, escorting troop convoys to attack isolated territories. The states with strong positions at maritime choke-points could use coastal forces to interrupt this traffic. In the Baltic, coastal forces were vital to integrate naval and military operations in an amphibious theatre, and elsewhere they were used to carry naval strength to the land, by bombardment and amphibious operations.

Naval battles in the age of the wooden sailing ship were rarely 'decisive', and so defeated fleets could easily retreat and refit, coming back within months to challenge the verdict of the last battle. It was only through the attrition of a succession of victories, allied to the administrative and economic collapse of the entire naval infrastructure, that a nation could be decisively defeated at sea.

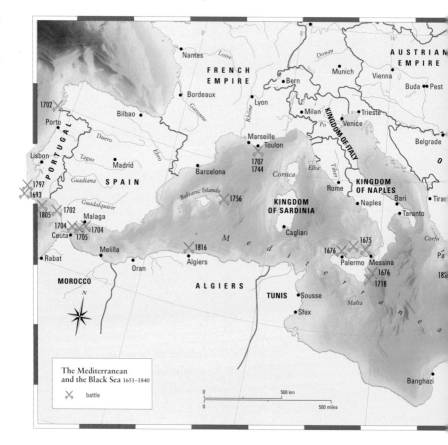

The Mediterranean and the Black Sea 1651–1840

✕ battle

SHIPS

The essential elements of warship design remained unaltered between 1650 and 1850. Ships were built of timber, and relied on canvas sails, controlled by hemp or manila ropes for motive power. Large ships used a three-masted rig with square sails on all masts. Smaller craft employed a variety of rigs, using one, two or three masts, with square and fore and aft sail plans. Each rig offered specific advantages of performance, ease of use, economy of manpower or suitability for particular conditions. Naval guns were smoothbore muzzle loaders cast from bronze or iron. Wrought-iron anchors with natural fibre cables were the usual ground tackle.

The largest ships, those intended for the 'line of battle' were properly called 'ships of the line', but the shorthand

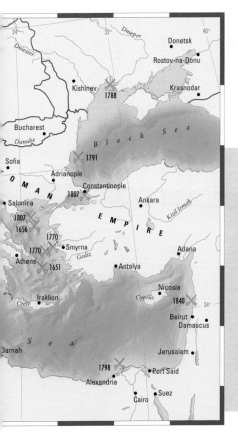

THE MEDITERRANEAN AND THE BLACK SEA 1651–1840

Commercial and strategic opportunities drew a number of powers into the Mediterranean, leading to a succession of wars involving France, Spain, Holland, Venice, Turkey, Russia, the Corsair states and ultimately the Americans. However, the British, while relative latecomers, won the key battles and secured bases at Gibraltar, Minorca and later Malta that enabled them to maintain control of the area.

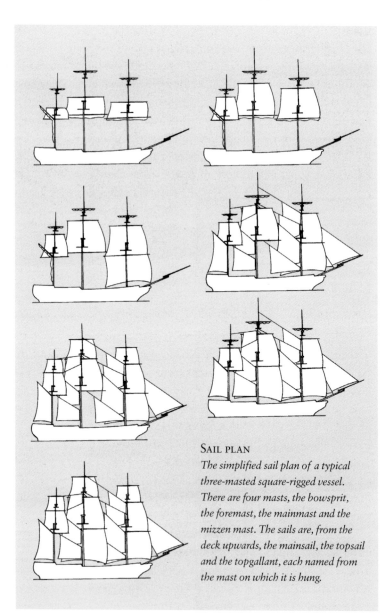

Sail plan

The simplified sail plan of a typical
three-masted square-rigged vessel.
There are four masts, the bowsprit,
the foremast, the mainmast and the
mizzen mast. The sails are, from the
deck upwards, the mainsail, the topsail
and the topgallant, each named from
the mast on which it is hung.

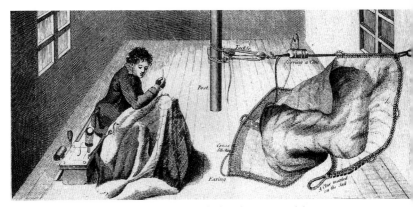

The manufacture of sails was another major dockyard process, with large rooms being set aside for this work, usually in the upper storeys of large buildings. Canvas, purchased on the open market, was brought into the dockyard to be cut and stitched into the particular sails for individual ships. Only in the nineteenth century were sails standardized.

'battleships' will be used here. They were intended to operate in fleets ands squadrons, emphasizing firepower and strength. Over time the base line for inclusion in the line of battle rose. In 1652 England and Holland used large numbers of hired merchant ships. By 1672 these had been removed, along with the smaller warships which lacked the structural strength to resist gunfire and the firepower to contribute to the fight. By the 1750s a 50-gun ship was a marginal battleship, but by the 1780s a 64-gunner was the lowest limit. Although the French and Spanish abandoned this type before the Revolutionary Wars, the British retained them, to keep up numbers and for trade defence. After 1805 the 74 was the smallest serious battleship, and by 1830 the basis for inclusion was 80 guns of the heaviest calibre.

Smaller units designed for superior speed were used for scouting and trade warfare. By the mid 1750s these had developed into the classic 'frigate', a single-decked warship. They were supported by diminutive sea-going types – sloops, corvettes and brigs. The basic requirement for a successful cruiser was the ability to capture a merchant ship.

Although some merchant ships, the large 'Indiamen' trading in the pirate-infested Indian Ocean, retained a significant armament until 1815, they rarely had the crew or motivation to fight. Small privateers were designed for superior speed and handiness. Their success in capturing their prey by boarding demonstrated the limits of self-defence.

The balance between battleships and cruisers, the size of ships built for each role, their armament and overall layout were determined by national priorities. Navies were more distinctive than contemporary armies, where regiments of infantry and cavalry, and the tally of artillery pieces could be compared numerically. At sea there were major national differences between ships of the same basic type, notably in stowage and armament per ton.

In the close fighting of the Anglo-Dutch wars, and later the Russo-Turkish conflicts, the fleet would be accompanied by fireships. These

A British sixth rate ship at Deptford dockyard in the 1770s. The flags and other activity indicate that she is about to be launched, stern first. In the foreground the raw material of shipbuilding has been unloaded to begin work on another vessel. Between the timber and the ship is a dry dock, into which this vessel might be taken, once launched, to have her hull copper-sheathed. (John Clevely the Elder)

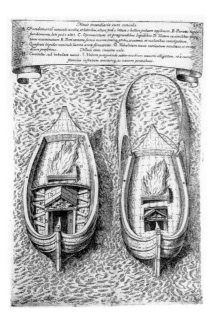

Between 1650 and 1700 the fireship was the most dangerous weapon afloat. It was the only small vessel that could destroy a large battleship and was often used to finish off disabled enemy vessels. Normally retaining their rig, they were navigated into position by a small crew of daring men. The Dutch were the masters of this tactic in the seventeenth century. Fireships and explosion vessels were used by the Russians in the 1770s, by Lord Cochrane in 1809 and by the Burmese and Chinese in the 1820s and 1830s.

small vessels were intended to grapple damaged enemy battleships and set them on fire. Inshore, the Baltic navies employed oared craft, initially based on the design of Mediterranean galleys, to combine firepower and mobility in shallow seas. Seapower navies also used oared gunboats for inshore operations, and from the 1680s employed bomb vessels to fire explosive shells into coastal cities.

In order to use their guns effectively, warships had to be relatively stable – that is, their motion had to be steady and predictable. They also had to be able to make good progress sailing into the wind – a task for which the heavy and manpower-intensive square rig was the best choice – and possess the seaworthiness to meet anticipated weather conditions. As the range and duration of major naval operations increased, wooden warships became larger (to carry the stores needed for the crew and the ship), and to improve their seaworthiness.

Each navy settled on a balance of qualities that met its particular needs. Short-ranged navies packed more firepower into a ship than those with global tasks; navies with shallow waters off their main bases required different ships to those with deep water anchorages. While the French attempted to introduce pure science into ship design, the basic problems of working with natural materials and imperfect structures ensured that wooden shipbuilding remained an art. While the British 'empirical' approach was equally successful, the fact that French ships designed by highly educated architects ended up gracing the list of His Britannic Majesty's navy demonstrated that their 'superiority' was often not enough to offset the seamanship and professionalism of British officers and men. French models were influential, but British ships were generally more strongly built, more durable, and better combat platforms.

SHIPBUILDING, TIMBER AND BASES

The limits of warship design were set by the timber from which they were built. Carrying and firing heavy guns imposed severe strains on the inherently flexible structure of the wooden ship. The design of

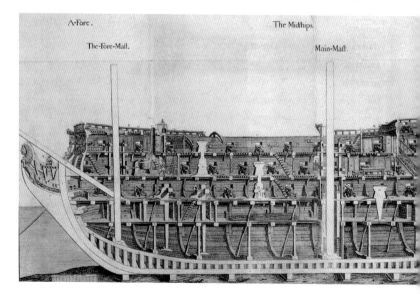

warships diverged from that of merchant ships because this structural load required a much stronger hull. Merchant ships stowed their heavy cargo low in the hold, but warships carried heavy guns high out of the water. This required a strongly built hull, which also enabled the ship to resist gunfire. The hull of the wooden warship developed into a massive structure, combining closely spaced longitudinal frames with thick horizontal planking laid edge to edge. The whole was secured by wooden nails. For 150 years the incremental increase in the size of ships, to meet the gradual expansion of strategic horizons, required no fundamental change in shipbuilding technology. However, the combination of long periods of sea service and ever greater loads imposed on the Royal Navy by the blockade strategy of the Revolutionary and Napoleonic Wars (1793–1815) led to the introduction of diagonal framing, and the use of wrought iron as a structural material. This new system facilitated a dramatic increase in the size of wooden warships, and eventually provided the strength to carry steam engines.

The preferred shipbuilding timber was oak, used for the hulls of most European and American warships. When fully seasoned, oak was durable, resistant to gunfire, and gave off fewer splinters than other woods. Although replaced by elm for planks below the waterline, and replaced altogether by Cuban mahogany and Indian teak in some

A contemporary section of an English first rate ship of the 1690s. With three covered gun decks, a commanding height out of the water and greater structural strength, the first rate formed the heart of the line of battle, and the ultimate arbiter of naval warfare. Fleets based around such ships sought command of the sea, while their value as deterrent and prestige symbols was immense.

THE SIZE OF SHIPS 1650–1850

	Length of Keel
Sovereign of the Seas (Built 1637)	127 ft (38.7m)
Rebuilt 1660	as *Royal Sovereign*
Rebuilt 1685	135.6 ft (41.4m)
Accidentally burned 1697	
Royal Sovereign II (Built 1701)	141.7 ft (43.2m)
Rebuilt 1728; broken up 1768	
Royal Sovereign III (Built 1774–86)	150.9 ft (46.0m)
Collingwood's flagship at Trafalgar; broken up 1841	
Royal Sovereign IV	
Ordered 1843 as 110-gun ship	166.6 ft (50.7m)
Laid down 1849 as 120-gun ship	172.6 ft (52.6m)
Launched 1857 as a steamship	201.0 ft (61.3m)
Converted into an armoured turret ship with nine guns in 1864–6	
Sold 1885	

The battle honours of this ship tell their own story: Kentish Knock 1652, St James's Day 1666, Sole Bay 1672, Schooneveld 1673, Texel 1673, Beachy Head 1690, Barfleur 1692, Glorious First of June 1794, Cornwallis's Retreat 1795, Trafalgar 1805. All but one were major contests for command of the sea.

Breadth	Tonnage
46.6 ft (14.2m)	1,522
47.6 ft (14.5m)	1605
48.4 ft (14.7m)	1,683
50.0 ft (15.2m)	1,868
52.1 ft (15.8m)	2,175
60.0 ft (18.2m)	3,019
60.0 ft (18.2m)	3,400
60.0 ft (18.2m)	3,765
	5,080

Although no ship saw service from 1650 to 1850, ships' names were reused. Sovereign of the Seas *of 1637 (below right) was Charles I's prestige flagship and the first three-decked battleship, representing England's claim to naval mastery. Rebuilt and renamed* Royal Sovereign *she established a tradition of naval mastery. (*Royal Sovereign II *fought in no major battles. Her role was primarily deterrent.)* Royal Sovereign III, *completed in 1786 (below left), carried Collingwood's flag at Trafalgar, and was the first to enter the battle.*

warships, oak remained the key timber. The peculiar demands of the wooden warship, which required huge curved timbers, or 'knees', to support the gun decks, ensured that straight, forest-grown trees had to be supplemented by the bent and gnarled products of exposed hedgerows or mountains. Masts and yards were made from softwoods, usually fir or pine. While many navies had indigenous supplies of oak, all the European navies required additional timber and masts. The main source for this timber, along with hemp, tar and pitch, were the great forests of the Baltic littoral, especially those of Poland and Russia. Naval bureaucrats relied on the local merchant communities, especially at Riga and Danzig, to supply naval stores of guaranteed quality. The Dutch Navy was largely built from Baltic timber, while the English and French depended on the Baltic forests for masts.

Structural strength was the key to the life of a wooden warship. Over time the frame and timbers would move, opening the joints to fresh water, which unlike salt, promoted decay. Unless the ship was docked, stripped down to the frame, and largely rebuilt, this process would accelerate, destroying the ship. The ability to rebuild ships, using dry docks, was a critical component of any long-term fleet programme. While well-built ships could, with regular reconstruction, last up to fifty years, their badly built sisters would be useless within half a decade.

The key to success was the use of carefully seasoned timber. Seasoning reduced the moisture content of the wood below 20 per cent, but required years of careful storage. In wartime it was impossible to maintain an adequate supply, forcing navies to use unseasoned or inferior timber. Under ideal conditions ships were built slowly from seasoned timber, allowing the frame and the hull to season at various stages before proceeding with further work. This took at least three years, and preferably twice as long. Yet in an emergency ships could be built in six months. However, building in haste with unseasoned timber was a recipe for disaster. Once the structure was closed, dark, warm and damp conditions promoted the rapid spread of fungal spores of

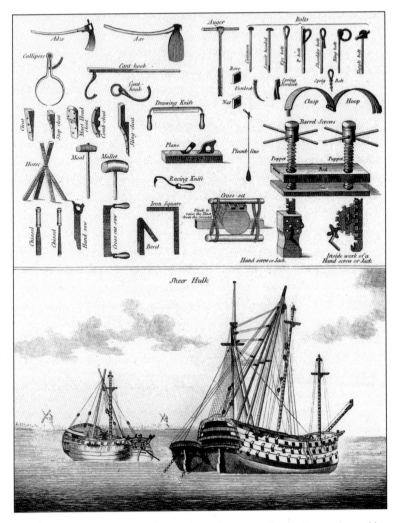

The tools required for mast making, and installing masts. Sheer hulks, cut-down old warships fitted with a pair of sheers, were used to hoist mainmasts up and lower them into the ship. Here a two-decker is receiving her mainmast, with the fore and mizzen already in place. To the left a ship is hoisting in her own masts, with jury-rigged sheers, a practice employed outside main bases.

'dry rot' which leeched out the strength of the timber, and destroyed the structural integrity of the ship. The antidote – excluding fresh water and providing for the free circulation of air and light – imposed a significant maintenance task on navies in peacetime.

Only navies with dry docks could maintain effective reserve fleets, through regular docking and inspection of the hull below the waterline. Consequently, the English built dry docks from 1495, perfecting the stone dry dock before 1700. France did not follow suit until the eighteenth century; the first dock at Brest opened in 1740, while Toulon did not have one until the 1770s. Sweden opened a dry dock in 1724, Denmark in 1739, and the United States Navy had to wait until 1833. Repairing ships without a dry dock required them to be hauled out of the water (which was only possible with relatively small ships), or heaved down on to one side while still afloat. Neither method was without danger.

Naval powers developed unique approaches to shipbuilding and repair. The British obsessions with the quality of materials generally secured a longer active life, making rebuilding economically attractive. The Russians built in haste, with ill-chosen materials, and kept up a steady rate of construction rather than rebuilding their ships. This made their naval policy look far more aggressive than it really was. By the nineteenth century, Britain, France and the United States all built slowly under cover and launched ships only when required. This was very expensive, requiring numerous covered slipways, but it produced the most durable wooden warships of all time, just as they became obsolete.

While timber quality and dry docks were vital to the active lives of warships, the development of bases around the docks provided the key to the operational use of navies. If a navy wanted to sustain operations in any theatre it had to have a local supply base from which it could draw masts, yards, sails, cordage, guns, ammunition, food, and replacement crew. Bases provided a secure anchorage for damaged ships, a rendezvous for seamen, and hospital facilities. Every time the English shifted their strategic horizons they built new and costly base facilities. By contrast, France preferred to surge squadrons into key theatres, and then send the ships home when they had accomplished their mission.

GUNS AND GUNNERY

Although heavy naval guns were capable of inflicting serious damage on ships, particularly their vulnerable masts and rigging (not to mention injuring the crew), they rarely sank large ships. It was this fact that made naval warfare tactically attritional. Only in the 1820s did new technology threaten to alter the balance. Before that the development of naval artillery had been steady and incremental. The size and length of naval guns was determined by the space available for recoil and the use of manpower to move and load them. In 1650 almost all naval guns were cast in bronze, and at the beginning of the eighteenth century it remained the best material for the purpose, being lighter and more durable than iron. When battle fleets began to expand, however, it was simply too expensive. The demands of armies, where lightness was at a premium, ensured that the cheaper cast-iron gun, pioneered by the English under Henry VIII, replaced bronze pieces for all but the smallest or most prestigious applications afloat after 1700. Throughout the era of the sailing ship, British iron guns were significantly stronger than those of their main rivals, a vital element in the superior rate of fire achieved by British gun crews. French iron guns frequently exploded, with catastrophic results. Russian, Swedish and American cast-iron guns were excellent.

The basis of naval gunnery was the need to fire rapidly at point-blank range (when the gun did not need to be elevated to make the range – normally around 200 yards or 180 metres), at 90 degrees to the keel, against similar ships. Individual aimed fire was of little use as a single shot could not sink or disable a ship. Naval gunnery doctrine reflected the same technical limitations as infantry volley fire, and the application of science to gunnery was a slow process. Experiments in the 1740s established the superiority of larger shot, and began to explore internal ballistics. More significantly, improved foundry practice in the 1760s meant that guns were no longer cast hollow. Instead they were cast solid, and then bored out by water- and later steam-powered lathes which provided a more accurate bore, enabling a more effective use of the powder. It also led to the development of the carronade in the 1770s by the Scottish Carron Company. (The same technology was critical to the success of James Watt's steam engine: his first cylinder was cast and bored at Carron.) Carronades fired a large calibre shot from a short, light gun, and replaced small calibre long guns on the upper decks of British warships. This greatly enhanced close-range firepower, and accentuated the Royal Navy's close-quarters combat doctrine.

Over time the weight of guns of each calibre was reduced, and the powder charge increased to enhance range and penetration. The choice of gun calibre varied. Britain, France, Russia and America favoured heavy guns on the lower decks of their battleships. But guns larger than 150 mm (6 inches), the British 32-pounder, were too heavy for sustained rapid fire. The British landed their last 180 mm 42-pounders in the 1780s, the French persevered with 36-pounders (nearly 40 imperial pounds) until the 1820s, while the Americans adopted the 42-pounder in 1815. By contrast, the 24-pounder was the heaviest gun in general use by the Dutch and Scandinavian navies.

The use of flintlocks to fire the guns from the 1780s increased the accuracy and regularity of fire. Later, gun sights and extensive training for gun crews, pioneered by Sir Philip Broke aboard HMS *Shannon*, inspired modern gunnery practice. By 1830 the British and French had

The battle of the Saintes, 12 April 1782. The French fleet under de Grasse, attempting to escort an army to conquer Jamaica, encountered the British under Rodney. A shift in the wind broke the French line, allowing superior British close-quarters firepower, notably from HMS Duke, a three-decked ship with flintlocks fitted to her cannon, to win a crushing victory. Six ships were taken. (Nicholas Pocock)

adopted a single calibre armament, with all guns firing the same calibre shot, either 30 or 32 pounds, although the guns on each deck were of different weights. At the same time the French artillerist Colonel Paixhans introduced a shell-firing gun. By 1850 battleships carried up to ten shell guns, usually of a larger calibre than the solid shot guns (200 mm or 8 inch). While the exploding shell promised a much enhanced ship-killing performance, the failure of the fuse and the inaccuracy of hollow projectiles restricted their value.

TACTICS

While sailing ship tactics have fascinated succeeding generations, the subject has an underlying simplicity. Tactical options were limited by the peculiarities of the sailing ship. In 1650 the leading naval power, the Dutch, favoured a close range mêlée action, but by 1672 the line of battle had been established as the standard formation, to maximize the use of heavy guns, and impose discipline on the fleet. As a basic building block for fleet operations the 'line ahead' proved fundamental. It set the standard of ship-handling required of naval officers, and provided a strong defensive formation. The massed firepower of a line could break up the enemy formation, inflicting crippling damage on individual ships, preparatory to a close-quarters engagement. Yet because ships could not advance and use their main armament at the same time, battles tended to be indecisive if both sides were roughly equal in size and skill. If the battle was going against the fleet sailing to the leeward in the defensive position, it had the choice of retreating. In the eighteenth century the French generally fought from the leeward position, as they were not seeking a decisive battle, and tried to cripple the masts and sails of the British ships so they could break off the engagement and pursue ulterior objects. Under these circumstances truly crushing victories were won only by fleets that were significantly larger, or significantly more skilful. For the British, the key to victory was to force the French to stand and fight. Essentially, they had to get to leeward of the French, denying them the option of retreat, and then concentrate a superior force on part of their formation. While the line of battle held this could be achieved using additional ships to double on the enemy, attacking from both sides. If the line could be broken, as at the Saintes in April 1782, the same effect could occur at the centre of the enemy line, where it would be more serious. If the enemy line collapsed, by accident or design, the resulting mêlée battle gave a great advantage to better trained and equipped forces. Nelson's dynamic tactics at Trafalgar attacked the cohesion of the Franco-Spanish line, relying on the superior skill and firepower of his ships to defeat the enemy at close quarters. Despite Nelson's example, the line would remain the basis of fleet tactics for as long as guns were the principal armament.

Although sea fighting made complex demands on senior officers, the transmission of the professional knowledge and understanding that are the basis of war at sea, usually termed 'doctrine', was still on a personal basis. This reflected the fact that admirals had to be experienced seamen before they could be effective commanders. In the Royal Navy each generation learnt the art of command from their elders and the hard experience of war. In the absence of formal naval education this practical teaching produced a succession of able commanders. In France a more scientific approach was adopted, and from the late seventeenth century naval tactics were analysed and reduced to theory. However, theory was no substitute for the development and transition of an effective, practical, naval doctrine.

A FLOATING SOCIETY

It is widely believed that service in sailing warships was a floating hell of tyrannical and sadistic officers, disgusting food and appalling conditions. This myth was created by liberal reformers in the 1830s to support their campaign to abolish the impressment of seamen and the use of physical punishment. The image was revived at the turn of the twentieth century by the poet John Masefield, and is sustained by the enduring image of Captain Bligh and the mutiny on the *Bounty*. In *The Wooden World*, his masterly examination of the inner life of the Royal

Navy in the mid eighteenth century, N. A. M. Rodger demonstrated that British success was based on an altogether more rounded and effective society in which the officers and men worked together, largely by consent. Furthermore, the navy was not a world apart, as Rodger tellingly observed: 'A ship's company, large or small, was a microcosm of society with a manifold division of ranks and ratings, of social classes and status, of skills and professions, and of ages. The life of the ship can only be understood in relation to these overlapping patterns.'

The analysis of 'a microcosm of society' can be applied to all navies. It helps to explain why some were more successful than others. Navies reflected the society from which they sprang, and the peculiar political and social patterns of every nation were mirrored afloat. Ashore, seamen were distinguished from the rest of society by their dress and habits. Afloat, they were marked out by their skill and initiative. Seamen learnt their trade at sea from an early age, acquiring the skill and strength to work aloft in the rigging while still in their teens. The true seamen, those who worked in the rigging, were vital to good sailing and safety in a storm. Aboard a battleship in wartime, such men would be diluted by non-seafarers, 'landmen', who could only work on deck. Landmen might, in time, become seamen. In wartime the sudden demand to double or treble the seafaring population could only be met by diluting naval and mercantile crews and using foreign seamen, released slaves, convicted smugglers and volunteers, together with men impressed from the seafaring community. While impressment was an infraction of civil liberties, it served the national good, and underpinned British mastery at sea. The French *Inscription Maritime*, which called up registered seafarers from a national list by rotation, was a theoretically superior system, but failed to deliver, and did nothing to recruit non-seafarers, who were vital to wartime expansion. Other nations limped along with bounty payments, coercion and versions of impressment. None ever solved the basic problem of naval manpower: how to double the number of sailors when war broke out, and maintain that level of manpower, despite heavy losses from disease and desertion.

Navies also employed soldiers, later marines, as small-arms men, landing parties, unskilled labour and, from the 1790s, as a barrier between the sailors and the officers. British marines were encouraged to go aloft by the lure of sailor's pay and status, which were considerably greater. Other vital elements in the naval service were the petty officers, skilled tradesmen like the gunner, the carpenter and the boatswain, and warrant officers like the sailing master, who was responsible for the navigation of the ship. In the Royal Navy the social divisions between officers and men were real but not impenetrable: James Cook signed on as an able seaman and died a captain. Elsewhere in society such mobility was rare.

Each nation had a naval officer corps that reflected the value they placed on the service. The British adopted professional standards in 1677, others took far longer. Some nations allowed army officers, privateers and foreigners to command afloat. Before 1793 the French officer corps was divided into two grades, and restricted to aristocrats, leaving the middle-class officers to form a separate caste. This was a static, restricted group. After the Revolution few experienced officers remained in service, weakening the combat-worthiness of a fleet where discipline had broken down. Sea officers required less personal wealth to further their careers than their military equivalents, and had significantly greater opportunities for personal gain. Prize money, for ships and cargoes captured, could transform the lives of successful officers. By the Napoleonic Wars the pursuit of 'honour' began to take precedence over financial reward. Nelson's career was marked by his subordination of prize to glory, while the American officers who fought the War of 1812 were obsessed with honour.

By contrast, the common concerns of seamen remained, first and foremost, financial. As the aristocrats of the pre-industrial labour market, mariners expected to be well paid. The reliable pay of the Royal Navy, and the high wages offered by the Dutch in the seventeenth century, contrasted with the repeated financial collapse of the French Navy, which was unable to retain men because it could not pay them. Beyond money, men were concerned to have a large supply of food and drink. Modern research suggests that the British naval diet provided a far better quality and quantity of food than was available to labourers ashore, averaging over 4,000 calories per day. While a diet of salt meat, dried peas, hard bread, dried fruit, beer and rum was not ideal, the lack of fresh vegetables and fruits being the prime cause of scurvy, it was substantial enough to fuel hard work. Furthermore, as navies ventured further afield they improved their ability to preserve food. This, like most other aspects of naval administration, required experienced men with adequate financial resources. Ultimately the British built dedicated victualling complexes at Deptford, Portsmouth and Plymouth to process animals and grain into salt meat, bread and beer ready to load aboard ship. Other nations, with less demanding strategic patterns, were not so lavish. The French fleet consistently failed to meet victualling needs, with disastrous results.

The greatest threat to life afloat was disease, as the overcrowded conditions aboard battleships provided ideal opportunities for the rapid spread of epidemics. Typhus or 'gaol fever' was common with newly raised crews that included pressed men, or non-seafarers, although the imposition of high standards of cleanliness aboard British ships made a major difference. Men were beaten for having dirty bodies or clothes, and 'unclean behaviour' – relieving themselves inboard rather than using the heads and piss-dales. 'Unclean behaviour' threatened the lives of all on board, but it was ignored in the Bourbon fleets, where officers showed remarkably little concern for the health and welfare of their men or the cleanliness of their ships. That the Royal Navy invested heavily in hospitals and medical practitioners was the best evidence that it took the health of the seamen seriously. This was not mere altruism, for in wartime seamen were always in short supply, so it made sense not to waste them.

A significant proportion of sailors suffered from venereal disease: during the Seven Years War an average of 8 per cent of sailors were treated every year. When a ship's company was paid off at a dockyard town, innkeepers and prostitutes were always on hand to relieve them of their new-found wealth. By the Revolutionary wars the fear of desertion

The theatre of punishment on board a Royal Navy warship around 1800. A man has been lashed to a grating (a hatch cover open for ventilation) to be flogged with the infamous 'cat-o'-nine-tails'. The marines are drawn up on the quarterdeck with loaded muskets, to ensure the punishment is carried out. Another man has stripped off his shirt, and is protesting that he, and not the man lashed up, is the real culprit.

was such that ships coming into harbour, even those going into dock, rarely gave shore leave. Consequently, captains arranged for a large party of 'wives', of the sort who had a 'husband in every ship', to be brought on board. The officers would then leave the crew to their own devices for a day or two. Those who recalled what then transpired only ever referred to scenes of debauchery beyond description. A more effective method of spreading venereal complaints could not be invented, but in the absence of effective methods of retaining men when reported there was no alternative. By contrast, homosexuality was relatively rare; when reported, it almost invariably led to capital punishment.

Naval punishments have long exerted a morbid fascination, with gruesome tales of 'keel-hauling' and 'flogging round the fleet' being served up to horrify the modern reader. In truth naval punishments mirrored those employed on shore. Physical chastisement or death were the usual options, with transportation to colonial empires an expensive alternative. There were few custodial sentences for working-class people ashore, and neither room nor reason for them afloat. Men were beaten, with the famous 'cat-o'-nine-tails', for offences ranging from drunkenness to desertion; mutiny and murder were punished by hanging at the yard arm. Thieves were forced to 'run the gauntlet', their shipmates beating them with the ends of knotted ropes. This reflected the particularly damaging effect of theft in the tight social fabric of the ship. There was no significant criticism of naval discipline until the 1830s, because there was no effective alternative. It is only in retrospect that flogging seems brutal. In the rough, physical world of the fighting sailing ship the men complained of arbitrary punishment, when officers were inconsistent, but not physical punishment itself. The bloodiest mutiny in the history of the Royal Navy occurred in 1797, when the crew of HMS *Hermione* butchered Captain Hugh Pigot and nine other officers, before taking the ship into a Spanish port. Their action followed an arbitrary reign of terror. It was sparked off by the death of two topmen who fell while hurrying to avoid a beating. Officers who treated their men as Pigot did were normally dismissed from the service. Despite that, the *Hermione* mutineers were hunted for a decade, and several were hanged. However, in most cases short of mutiny seamen were too valuable to be beaten senseless, or hanged, if some other punishment could be found. Stopping their rum ration was a useful coercive measure.

Naval punishment was conducted as a ceremony. Offenders were dealt with in public, with the rest of the crew watching, the theatrical display being intended to serve as a deterrent. Often men would be prepared for execution, and pardoned at the last moment. British naval punishment was regulated by the *Articles of War* which restricted a captain to awarding a dozen lashes, although up to thirty-six were issued as a multiple punishment. Captains' log books were regularly checked to see that they were not awarding excessive floggings. The unfortunate William Bligh, so well known through caricature performances on film, was not a tyrant. His problems stemmed from his lowly social status, insufficient personal authority, the lack of a marine detachment on the *Bounty*, excessive leniency at Tahiti and a foul temper.

Over time, the relationship between officers, petty officers and men in the Royal Navy altered. The French Revolution marked a significant step in the introduction of a rigid hierarchy to replace the older consensual approach. Nations with less flexible social patterns found seamen difficult to handle. During the Seven Years War the British introduced the 'Divisional System', which made each officer personally responsible for the well-being of a number of the men. This helped to bond the crew together. Good officers took their duties seriously, protecting their men's rights, ensuring the sick were cared for, and passing their property to their families if they died. The system also allowed officers to control the cleanliness of the men and of their clothes and hammocks, to exercise them at their guns and other drills, and to help train the novices.

The sailor remained a resource to be drawn from the market when required until the end of the sailing ship era. British sailors were signed on for the commission of the ship, a period of normally three years but often longer in wartime. Once they were paid off, they and all the training and experience they had obtained were lost to the service. The introduction of continuous service for seamen gunners trained at HMS *Excellent* in the 1830s, with men signed on for ten years, was an innovation soon copied by other navies to recover the investment made in training. Such men soon came to form the nucleus of any new crew. By 1850 the major navies were already moving away from the age-old systems of recruiting seamen for service on one commission, or one voyage. By the 1870s the warship sailor had become a different creature to his mercantile cousin; he served for a term of years, often twenty, had a pension and a real career structure, and specialized in the technical aspects of his work.

Life afloat mirrored that ashore, with the added dangers of death by drowning and shipboard diseases. However, a naval career offered the hope of advancement for many and excitement for all. With careful administration its rigours could be ameliorated.

CHAPTER TWO

The Anglo-Dutch Wars and the Origins of Modern Naval Power 1650–74

The Four Days battle, 1–4 June 1666. A detail from Storck's painting showing the stern of Admiral de Ruyter's flagship Zeven Provincien *on the first day. After four days the Dutch had won an impressive victory, but within the month the English had more than made up for their defeat. Such close and frequent main fleet actions were the main feature of the three Anglo-Dutch wars. The artist was familiar with the Dutch, but not the English, ships. Storck, like his contemporaries, also compressed events in space and time, producing a packed canvas. (Abraham Storck)*

The Anglo-Dutch Wars and the Origins of Modern Naval Power 1650–74

THE ANGLO-DUTCH wars of the mid seventeenth century established the form and substance of war at sea for the next two centuries. Not only were they the most 'maritime' wars of the era, being struggles for commerce rather than territory, with no land fighting in the main theatre, but they were fought with an intensity unequalled in any subsequent conflict. They shaped the development of the English Royal Navy, witnessed the creation of the modern French Navy and wore down the hitherto dominant fleet of the United Netherlands. The ship types and tactics that evolved remained at the core of naval warfare until steam replaced sail in the 1850s.

In 1650 the Dutch were the acknowledged masters of naval warfare. Their powerful maritime economy and long war with Spain had created a unique force. The republic depended on the North Sea herring fishery and trade with the Baltic for its survival, and it profited from distant voyages to the Mediterranean, the West Indies and the East Indies. The Dutch dominated the European carrying trades and the provision of shipping services. Much of England's trade was carried by Dutch ships, even that between the American colonies and the homeland. Maritime activity provided the Dutch with a large fleet of armed merchant ships for war service. The free use of the sea was the guiding principle of their commercial existence, a concept given legal form in Hugo Grotius's *Mare Liberum* of 1609, although John Selden's *Mare Clausum Seu Dominium Maris* of 1635 reasserted the old English claim to rule the narrow seas, and demand a salute from all passing shipping.

Dutch naval tactics emphasized speed, manoeuvre and boarding. They relied on superior sailing and close-quarters fighting to break up enemy formations, board disabled ships and use fireships. These advantages had been exploited to the full by the leading Dutch admiral, Maerten Harpertszoon Tromp (1597–1653), when he routed the Spanish at the battle of the Downs in 1639. Tromp, the last great naval commander of the age of mêlée battles, was first and foremost a seaman. He was idolized by his men, and respected by the English. Dutch warships were lightly armed, although Tromp's flagship, the *Brederode*, mounted fifty-nine guns; the next largest ship had forty-eight, while most had only thirty guns. Although the shoal waters of the Dutch coast required shallow draft, the relatively light armament of the Dutch ships actually reflected the need to operate far afield. The Dutch had built a cruiser fleet to protect their shipping from Spanish privateers, organized locally in five separate provincial admiralties, and paid for by taxes on merchant ships and their cargoes. This direct link between the navy and the service it was intended to perform paralleled that between contemporary armies and tax gathering. As the five admiralties had fluctuating incomes, their contribution to the national effort at sea was variable, while their rivalries affected the conduct of war.

A Dutch frigate. Smaller warships of this type were used for scouting, escort and other work outside the line of battle. Their design stressed seaworthiness and speed, rather than firepower. The Dutch, with their wide maritime interests, required more of these cruising ships than the English.

The English merchant marine, smaller and more specialized than that of the Dutch, was dominated by fishing and the Newcastle–London coal trade. England's share of the annual Newfoundland cod fishery produced ocean-going mariners, while commerce in high-risk areas, like the Corsair-infested Mediterranean, relied on heavily built, armed and well-manned ships. These could not compete with the Dutch in the secure waters of the Baltic and North Sea. In 1648 peace with Spain removed the last barrier to Dutch commercial shipping, which rapidly recaptured markets lost to the English. However, the new English Commonwealth government was closely linked to the commercial classes by shared political interests and a large state debt. Half a century of anti-Dutch propaganda, reflecting their dominance of the herring fishery, whaling, colonial trades and the 'massacre' of British merchants at the Indonesian Island of Amboyna in 1623 bore fruit in the Navigation Act of August 1651. This was designed to cut the Dutch out of the carrying trade between England and her colonies and the *entrepôt* trade with the Baltic, limit Dutch fishing on the English coast and protect English shipping in the East Indies. The pretext for war was the age-old claim that England ruled the Channel. In 1652 the English fleet was already at sea, dealing with Royalist privateers.

THE FIRST ANGLO-DUTCH WAR 1652–4

Recognizing the threat implicit in the Navigation Act, the Dutch increased their naval taxes by one third in 1650, and mobilized 150 warships and armed merchantmen in early 1652 to protect their shipping in European waters. Inevitably, in May came the clash over the English claim to a salute off Dover, involving Tromp and the English general-at-sea Robert Blake (1598–1657), in which the Dutch lost two ships. The real issue was the English claim of a right to search Dutch ships for French goods. The Dutch argued that the neutrality of the ship covered the goods it carried, while the British claimed that the ownership and nature of the cargo determined whether it was a prize of war. In essence, the Dutch wanted to use the sea, the English to control it, and deny it to others. This basic difference, fundamental to the strategic value of the sea, led to endless disputes between the English and the Dutch, the French and the Americans. In 1652 neither the English nor the Dutch were prepared to compromise.

The Commonwealth was confident that it would win. The navy had been critical to the Parliamentary victory in the Civil War, and it was now the first line of defence for the regime against continental support for the Stuart cause. In contrast to the Dutch fleet, the English Navy had built on the Tudor legacy of large, purpose-built warships carrying a heavy battery of large calibre guns. It had been designed to assert command of the short seas, sacrificing operational range, agility and speed for steadiness and all-round fighting strength. There were eighteen ships with more than forty guns, including the *Sovereign of the Seas*, the largest ship afloat, which carried 100 guns on three decks. Richly ornamented, as the symbol of the power and prestige of the Stuart state, she was too large and drew too much water to be an ideal component in the mixed fleets of the First War, yet the Dutch were awestruck by the firepower of the 'Golden Devil'. In general, English warships and merchant ships were bigger, more heavily armed, and, of equal importance, more heavily built, than their rivals. This would give them a critical advantage if the war at sea was dominated by artillery.

The English strategy was simple. By controlling the Channel and the Dutch coast they could impose a blockade, cut Dutch trade and rely on economic dislocation in Holland and Zealand to secure a settlement. The war would be short and limited to the sea. The English object was trade, not territory. The fleet was commanded by Parliamentary generals-at-sea, appointed to impose order and discipline on the fleet, notably Robert Blake and George Monck (1608–70). The English had a further advantage in their unified service and administration.

Before the war Tromp advised the States-General, the Dutch parliament, to collect a great fleet suitable for the mêlée tactics he still favoured, observe the English, and attack them as soon as possible.

THE WAR ZONE

The decisive struggle was for command of the sea lanes of northern Europe. The English strategy was to cut the Dutch off from their trade, and strangle their economy.

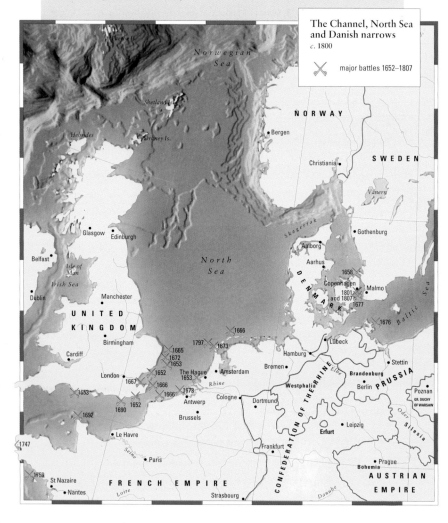

The Channel, North Sea
and Danish narrows
c. 1800

✗ major battles 1652–1807

NORWAY

• Bergen

SWEDEN

• Christiania

Vänern

• Gothenburg

Skagerrak

Aalborg

North
Sea

Aarhus

1658

DENMARK

Copenhagen • Malmö
1801
and 1807
1677

1676 Baltic Sea

Glasgow • Edinburgh

Belfast

Isle of
Man

Irish Sea

Dublin   Manchester

UNITED
KINGDOM

• Birmingham

Cardiff

London •

1653

1667

1652

1692

1690

1747

1759 St Nazaire
• Nantes

1666
1797 1673
1665
1672
1653
1652
The Hague
1653 • Amsterdam
1666
1666 1673
Antwerp

• Le Havre

FRENCH EMPIRE

Seine • Paris

Loire

Strasbourg

Lübeck

Hamburg

Bremen

• Amsterdam
Rhine

Brussels

Cologne Dortmund

Westphalia

CONFEDERATION OF THE RHINE

Frankfurt

Erfurt

Elbe

Brandenburg

Berlin PRUSSIA

• Leipzig

Danube

Stettin

Poznan

GR. DUCHY
OF WARSAW

Oder

Silesia

• Prague
Bohemia

AUSTRIAN

EMPIRE

Norwegian
Sea

Faeroe Is.

Shetland Is.

Hebrides

Orkney Is.

Confident that a major victory would secure a favourable political settlement, Tromp sought out Blake's fleet which was attacking the herring fishery off Scotland, only to lose a dozen ships in a gale and be recalled in disgrace. However, the incoming Dutch East India ships were able to slip past the English, and Michiel de Ruyter (1607–76) won a small action in the Channel. Without Tromp the Dutch were heavily defeated by Blake in a two-day battle off the Kentish Knock on 8 October, but escaped with the loss of only three ships. Tromp was reinstated and ordered to escort 450 merchant ships down the Channel, and then return with an inbound convoy. Leaving his convoy behind, Tromp severely mauled Blake's smaller fleet on 10 December off Dungeness, opening the Channel for his convoys. The story that he proceeded down the Channel with a broom at the mast-head of his flagship, to symbolize having 'swept' the English from the seas, is without foundation. Defeat galvanized the English, who reinforced their fleet to nearly eighty ships and prepared to meet Tromp on his return.

In a running battle off Portland between 28 February and 2 March 1653, English firepower and discipline proved decisive. Tromp attacked and pushed his convoy through, but in the process lost a dozen warships and forty-three merchant ships. He was weakened by the indiscipline of his captains, at least twenty of whom failed to fight. The English had regained command of the Channel. Nothing daunted, Tromp returned with an even larger fleet and engaged Monck and Deane off the Gabbard Shoal on 2 June, but when Blake's division joined on the following day, the Dutch were routed, losing seventeen ships. The English then blockaded the Dutch coast, causing serious economic damage. Tromp came out with over 100 ships in early August to break the blockade, engaging Monck off Scheveningen on 10 August. After Tromp was killed early in the battle much of the fight went out of the Dutch, who limped back into port with the loss of eleven ships. The English were little better off: although they only lost one ship, thirty-five were so heavily damaged that Monck had to lift the blockade.

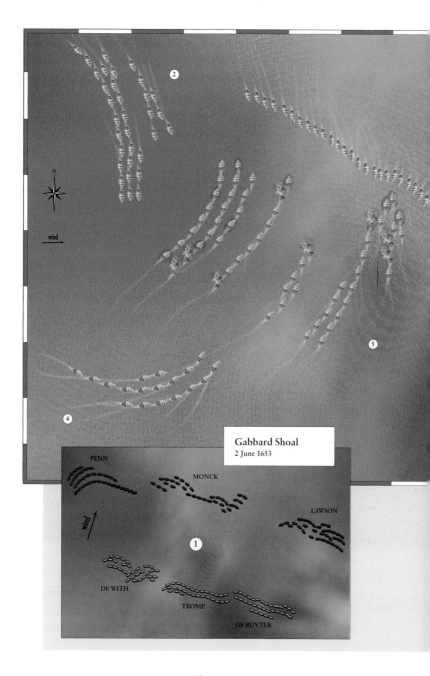

Gabbard Shoal
2 June 1653

PENN

MONCK

LAWSON

wind

DE WITH

TROMP

DE RUYTER

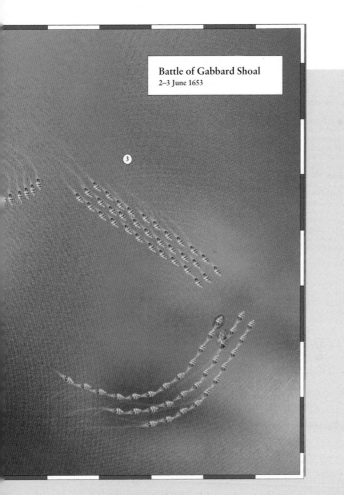

Battle of Gabbard Shoal
2–3 June 1653

1. 9–10 am, 2 June: an English fleet of 100 ships commanded by generals-at-sea Monck and Deane slowly overhaul a Dutch fleet of 98 ships under Admiral Maerten Tromp

2. 11 am, 2 June: as the action begins English general-at-sea Deane is killed

3. 6 pm, 2 June: fighting continues until the Dutch fleet hauls off having lost four ships

4. Early hours, 3 June: eighteen English ships commanded by Robert Blake arrive and try to position themselves between the Dutch ships and their home bases

5. 3 June: under light winds the two fleets face each other and open fire at midday. After four hours, the Dutch break off in a state of confusion, with eleven ships captured (shown ringed on map) and a further nine sunk. The English lose no ships

At Scheveningen the English first formally employed the 'line of battle' to maximize the tactical power of artillery, and minimize Dutch seamanship. As the big English ships were too unwieldy to put about and use both broadsides, they used the line as a defensive formation, building tactics on military discipline and the effective service of artillery. This was hardly surprising, as the generals were experienced gunners. The development of the line was critical to the effective use of large, gun-armed warships. It was not an intellectual breakthrough, merely the application of a soldier's common sense to the problem of maximizing firepower. The linear battle was already well established on land. For the new tactic to be effective each 'ship of the line' needed firepower and strength, as well as discipline. Captains were subject to severe penalties if they broke formation, and consequently merchant ships and merchant captains were removed from the battle fleet. Only a purpose-built war fleet commanded by professional naval officers under strict discipline could exploit the new tactics. It did not matter that the line of battle was not an effective attacking tactic — ships could not advance and fire — because in the first two Anglo-Dutch wars the superior strategic position of the English enabled them to cut Dutch trade and force them to attack.

After Scheveningen the Dutch managed to turn round a huge Baltic convoy. While this kept their economy from collapse in 1653, the prospects for the new year were poor. Reliant on imported shipbuilding materials and artillery, the Dutch could not replace their losses, let alone build the new ships needed to meet the English. The war ended because Cromwell, who became Lord Protector in late 1653, did not approve of fighting fellow Protestants. The Treaty of Westminster upheld the Navigation Laws, but dropped many of the more ambitious English claims including taxing the fishery. Outside the Channel the Dutch had swept the seas of English shipping, but the loss of 1,500 Dutch merchant ships in the Channel and North Sea had been decisive.

The English Navy was now three times larger than it had been under Charles I. The unprecedented shipbuilding, infrastructure and manpower demands reflected the English determination to seize a significant part of the world's trade from the Dutch. Having created an instrument of European significance, Cromwell used it to improve the security of British trade in the Mediterranean. Blake chastised the North African pirates in 1654–5, and then forced trade concessions from Portugal. Cromwell then found strong commercial and religious reasons to attack Spain. The war lasted from 1656 to 1659, and although the capture of Jamaica and Blake's great victory at Santa Cruz were notable achievements, Spanish privateers, used to preying on the Dutch, crippled English merchant shipping. This, added to the indecisive nature of the 1654 settlement, created the basis for further Anglo-Dutch conflict. English and Dutch interests clashed in the Baltic and the East Indies, while the Anglo-Spanish war allowed Dutch shipping back into many trades from which it had been excluded. By the late 1650s the protection of merchant shipping had become a major strategic task for the English Navy.

The Restoration of the English monarchy in 1660 added a new complication. Although the English state was financially weak, Charles II wanted to create an absolutist regime which would function without the interference of Parliament. A Dutch war appeared to be a promising commercial opportunity, in that a large financial indemnity would pave the way for the establishment of Stuart autocracy, and satisfy an impoverished aristocracy. Many shared the confidence of Monck (now Earl of Albemarle), that having beaten the Dutch once it would be easy enough to do so again.

English commercial horizons were extended in 1662 when Charles II accepted Tangier and Bombay as the dowry of his Portuguese queen, Catherine of Braganza. Tangier proved ill-suited to trade, and a source of endless conflict with the Moors. It was abandoned in 1683. Bombay, given to the East India Company, developed into the foremost naval station in the Indian Ocean. Together with colonies in North America and the West Indies, these new possessions began to stretch English seapower around the globe in support of trade.

THE SECOND ANGLO-DUTCH WAR 1665-7

A new war escalated out of colonial disputes on the West African slave coast, which involved the financial interests of the king, his brother James, Duke of York (the Lord High Admiral), and other prominent Royalists. In 1664 James sent an expedition to capture the Dutch American settlement of New Amsterdam, which was promptly renamed New York. Dutch shipping was attacked in European waters from late 1664, and Charles II finally declared war in March 1665.

After 1654 the Dutch, led by John de Witt, the Grand Pensionary of Holland, rebuilt their fleet and imposed greater discipline on their officers, although they were still divided into five regional squadrons. The naval balance had shifted. The Dutch now had more 'ships of the line', but none mounting more than 76 guns, and still relied on close action and boarding rather than firepower. The English fleet included eight big three-decked ships of 80–100 guns. The fleet would be centrally controlled. James had developed the linear concept of 1653 by giving each ship her place in the line and dividing the fleet into three divisions: van, centre and rear, under white, red and blue flags respectively. He also issued *Fighting Instructions*, which emphasized the importance of preserving a coherent, mutually supporting line, that would give the firepower to break up the enemy formation and open the way for exploitation. Like the generals-at-sea, James had considerable military experience, and did not favour leaving the initiative to his subordinates.

The initial English blockade, commanded by James, lasted only a fortnight before the fleet ran short of provisions and was forced to put back into the Thames estuary. This allowed Opdam, the Dutch commander, to collect his forces and seek out the enemy.

Each fleet had approximately one hundred ships. They met off Lowestoft on 13 June. The English had the weather gauge (the wind favouring them), and bore down on the Dutch at daybreak. Opdam rushed into battle without forming a line, and suffered considerable damage. The two fleets then passed on opposite tacks, firing as they went. Neither fleet managed to form a true line, being bunched and confused, the Dutch rather more than the English. Both sides then tacked and made another pass; the English tacked again after this pass, and were now on the same course as the Dutch, allowing the battle to settle down into an artillery duel. Opdam's *Eendracht* and James's *Royal Charles* were locked in close combat until mid afternoon, when the Dutch ship blew up. Sandwich, in the English van, then led his squadron through a gap in the Dutch line, while Prince Rupert closed with the Dutch rear. This combination of disaster and pressure broke the Dutch formation and they ran for home. Although they lost seventeen ships and 5,000 men, the Dutch were fortunate to escape, as the English pursuit was delayed by an unauthorized signal.

The victory was largely wasted. Rather than reimpose the blockade, the English vainly attempted to plunder Dutch convoys. The Plague in London, and the chronic weakness of the English finances, made it impossible to keep the fleet fully victualled and manned throughout the summer.

In early 1666 France declared war on England, complicating the strategic picture. For the new season Charles kept James, the heir to the throne, at Court, leaving Albemarle and Prince Rupert in joint command. They were ordered to divide their fleet following erroneous intelligence that the French Toulon squadron was about to enter the Channel. Rupert took twenty of the most powerful ships to meet this imaginary threat, leaving Albemarle with fifty-six to face ninety-two Dutch ships under de Ruyter.

Albemarle moved into the Thames estuary to wait for the Dutch, and for Rupert. Early on 11 June he found the Dutch anchored off the North Foreland and, during a hasty council of war, persuaded his captains to attack, rather than make for safety in the Swin anchorage, thus opening what became known as the Four Days battle. Surprised by the English attack, the Dutch were unable to exploit their advantage of superior numbers. Although the impetuous, undisciplined assault of the White Division under Admiral Berkeley led not only to the loss of

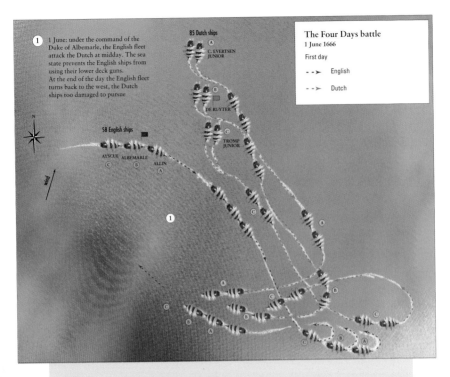

The Four Days battle
1 June 1666

First day

- - → English
- - → Dutch

1 1 June: under the command of the Duke of Albemarle, the English fleet attack the Dutch at midday. The sea state prevents the English ships from using their lower deck guns.
At the end of the day the English fleet turns back to the west, the Dutch ships too damaged to pursue

85 Dutch ships

C. EVERTSEN JUNIOR

DE RUYTER

TROMP JUNIOR

58 English ships

AYSCUE   ALBEMARLE

ALLIN

wind

N

THE FOUR DAYS BATTLE 1–4 JUNE 1666

Concerned that the French fleet, allied to the Dutch, was about to enter the Channel, the English fleet under Albemarle and Prince Rupert was divided. Despite this Albemarle engaged de Ruyter and fought for two days before Rupert rejoined. Poor discipline cost the English the battle, and a number of ships when impetuous captains rushed into battle without support.

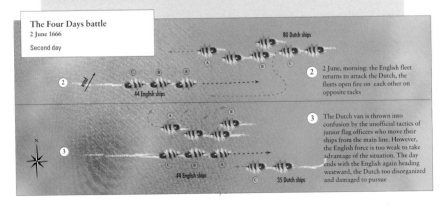

The Four Days battle
2 June 1666

Second day

80 Dutch ships

wind

44 English ships

2 2 June, morning: the English fleet returns to attack the Dutch, the fleets open fire on each other on opposite tacks

N

44 English ships

35 Dutch ships

3 The Dutch van is thrown into confusion by the unofficial tactics of junior flag officers who move their ships from the main line. However, the English force is too weak to take advantage of the situation. The day ends with the English again heading westward, the Dutch too disorganized and damaged to pursue

three ships and the disabling of two more but to Berkeley's death, the Dutch lost Admiral Evertsen and had two ships burned, while two of their admirals were forced to shift their flags into fresh ships when their original vessels were disabled.

On the second day Albemarle's fleet had the better of the fighting, largely driving off the Dutch, before de Ruyter pulled them together and pursued the retiring English. Late on the third day Rupert, who had only belatedly heard of the Dutch advance, came in sight to the west, and as Albemarle manoeuvred to join him the imposing *Royal Prince* went aground, and was burnt by the Dutch. That evening the English admirals agreed to attack the following day. Although de Ruyter still had sixty-four ships, many were battered and their crews were exhausted. The English had twenty fresh ships. However, Rupert wasted the advantage with an ill co-ordinated and impetuous attack, which left his flagship and her seconds crippled when a more careful

The grounded Royal Prince *surrenders to the Dutch on 3 June 1666, the third day of the Four Days battle. This famous old ship had been James I's prestige vessel, and remained a powerful symbol of the Stuart monarchy. The loss of the ship, which was eventually burnt by the Dutch, was the most serious blow inflicted during the battle. (Van de Velde the Younger)*

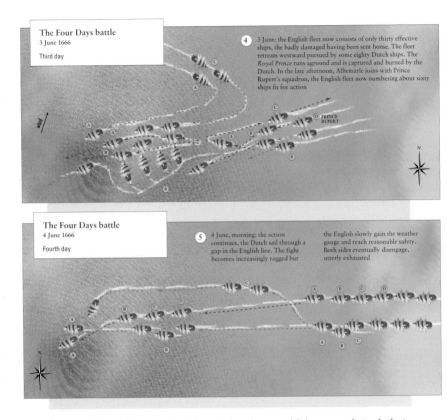

The Four Days battle
3 June 1666

Third day

3 June: the English fleet now consists of only thirty effective ships, the badly damaged having been sent home. The fleet retreats westward pursued by some eighty Dutch ships. The *Royal Prince* runs aground and is captured and burned by the Dutch. In the late afternoon, Albemarle joins with Prince Rupert's squadron, the English fleet now numbering about sixty ships fit for action

The Four Days battle
4 June 1666

Fourth day

4 June, morning: the action continues, the Dutch sail through a gap in the English line. The fight becomes increasingly ragged but the English slowly gain the weather gauge and reach reasonable safety. Both sides eventually disengage, utterly exhausted

approach, relying on the line of battle, would have exploited their superior firepower. Consequently, the English lost another ship that day, and finally retreated when mist began to shroud the area. The English had been beaten, losing prizes and prisoners to the Dutch, but both fleets were too shattered to continue the fight.

On 4 August 1666, St James's Day, the fleets met again; the English, reinforced by the *Royal Sovereign*, had eighty-nine ships, the Dutch eighty-eight. Despite de Ruyter's skilful fighting retreat, the Dutch were badly beaten. Ten days later Admiral Holmes demonstrated the nature of English mastery, making a 'bonfire' of 150 merchant ships at Vlie. The French never joined their allies.

In England the Great Fire of London, added to a general war-weariness and lack of money, increased pressure for peace. In early 1667 Charles, assured that the French would not attack and expecting peace, decided not to fit out the fleet, ignoring signs of Dutch activity. De Ruyter then attacked Chatham, capturing the fleet flagship *Royal Charles* (previously Cromwell's *Naseby*) and burning several other ships. The capture of the flagship, part of which still graces the Rijksmuseum in Amsterdam, was the high point of Dutch naval success, and it was only possible because the English fleet had not been mobilized. The peace of Breda, signed on 21 July, accepted the Dutch definition of contraband of war, and allowed them to carry the produce of Germany and the Spanish Netherlands (modern Belgium) to England.

THE THIRD ANGLO-DUTCH WAR 1672–4

After the war Anglo-Dutch relations improved, largely in response to the threat posed by the continental ambitions of Louis XIV's France. Yet Charles still hoped to emulate his French cousin, creating an autocratic regime independent of Parliament. Louis exploited his hope, as well as Charles's covert Catholicism, to purchase a secret alliance in

A royal humiliation. When the bankrupt Stuart administration could not afford to fit out the battle fleet in 1667, expecting peace, the Dutch penetrated the difficult Medway navigation in mid June and, despite the best efforts of the English, burnt ships and carried away the English flagship from Chatham. Their reward was an improved peace. The Stuart state could not afford a long war with so expensive a weapon as a battle fleet. (J. Peeters)

1670. Charles also raised money from Parliament, promising to strengthen the fleet against the French, but instead used it to wage war on the Dutch in alliance with France. While the war was variously attributed to the insult of having the *Royal Charles* on public display, and failure to salute a royal yacht, these were only pretexts. Charles wanted a war, and although he knew it would be unpopular gambled on a decisive campaign before Parliament reassembled to secure a profitable peace and silence his domestic opponents. But he had underestimated the Dutch. The war began with a bungled attack on a Dutch channel convoy in March 1672, but the Dutch had little time to celebrate before French armies swept into their country. Only the water defences of Holland and Zealand held them. If the Dutch lost at sea they would be doomed. Once again they entrusted their fleet to de Ruyter, the greatest admiral of the age, and he did not disappoint them. De Ruyter would use the linear battle as the basis of a defensive strategy, frustrating the efforts of the larger allied fleet to force a decisive action. He opened his campaign by seeking out the English, hoping to attack them before the French joined them.

Although he was too late, on 28 May de Ruyter attacked the combined fleet of seventy-four ships anchored in Sole Bay under James, Duke of York, with his own force of sixty-two ships. This was the most closely fought action of the three wars. The allies were able to get under way before the Dutch came into contact, but, with limited sea room and shoal waters, the French tacked to the south, rather than following the English squadrons to the north. This enabled twenty Dutch ships to contain thirty heavy French ships. De Ruyter, following the usual convention, ordered his flagship to engage James's *Royal Prince*, which was eventually disabled, as was the next ship James boarded, the *St Michael*. James ended the day aboard yet another three-decker, the *London*. At the northern end of the line Admiral van Ghent concentrated his assault on the crippled *Royal James*, the flagship of Lord Sandwich. The *Royal James* was destroyed by fireships, and the corpulent Sandwich drowned while attempting to shift his flag.

The loss of the admiral and a prestigious flagship gave the honours of the day to the Dutch, leading to much criticism of the French (who had done nothing wrong) by those who opposed the war. De Ruyter's spoiling attack hampered the development of allied strategy, both the attack on Dutch commerce, and the amphibious operations designed to turn the Dutch land defences. It was not enough to save the Dutch regime, however. Grand Pensionary John de Witt was lynched and the Stadtholderate renewed for William of Orange, who revitalized the land war.

By contrast, Charles had to recall Parliament, and accept their terms to secure the funds to carry on his war. The prevailing anti-Catholic mood forced James to come ashore once more, leaving Rupert in command. In 1673 de Ruyter again failed to prevent a junction of the allied fleets. This time he withdrew to the Schooneveld, a channel running along the coast off Walcheren, to await the allies. The king, the Duke of York and Prince Rupert decided to attack to clear the way for an invasion. When battle was joined on 28 May, de Ruyter had fifty-two ships to oppose seventy-six significantly larger allied ships. The honours went to de Ruyter, who had avoided defeat by a greatly superior force. On 14 June he began the second battle of the Schooneveld, driving the allied fleet back to Sole Bay. De Ruyter then tacked back to his old anchorage, having effectively stalled the allies.

The final action of the Anglo-Dutch wars was fought off the Texel on 11 August 1673, when de Ruyter was ordered to sea to protect the coast from an invasion, rumoured to be 30,000 strong (in fact there were only 6,000 troops on hand) and to cover the inbound shipping. This time eighty-six allied ships faced sixty Dutch. Poor English gunnery contributed to yet another Dutch success. That the English chose to blame the French for the failure said more about the national view of the war than the actual conduct of the battle. By this stage public opinion had shifted decisively. In the interval a major Dutch raid on New York and the Newfoundland fisheries exposed British weakness. The Second Treaty of Westminster reflected the failure of the

The Dutch fleet closing in on Admiral Spragge's damaged flagship Prince *at the battle of the Texel, 11 August 1673.* Cornelis Tromp's Gouden Leeuw *leads, while Prince Rupert in the* Royal Sovereign *can be seen in the distance between the two ships. Tromp and Spragge fought out a private battle, until Spragge was drowned when the boat he was using to shift his flag for a second time was sunk. (Van de Velde the Younger)*

war at sea. Despite their desperate situation the Dutch merely recognized Charles's claim to the salute, and paid him £200,000. His subjects did rather better, exploiting their neutral status to profit from the war between France and Holland which continued until 1679.

The relatively badly manned English fleet of 1672–3 emphasized the need to impose professional standards and discipline, and in 1677 the Royal Navy introduced professional qualifications for sea officers. In order to secure a lieutenant's commission the applicant had to be at least 20 years old, have three years' sea experience and pass an examination by a board of senior captains. These regulations were intended to close the gap between the experienced middle-class seamen, often called 'tarpaulins', and the young, enthusiastic, but unskilled and ill-disciplined 'gentlemen'. At the Four Days battle impetuous attacks by 'gentlemen' threw away the advantages of superior firepower and the line without need or thought. At the same time unemployed officers received 'half-pay' as a form of retainer. The system of 'impressment' exploited the traditional right of the state to command the service of mariners. By contrast the Dutch had to hire Germans, Norwegians and even English seamen to man their ships. This only exacerbated the lack of a national identity in the chaos of Dutch naval administration.

Because the Navigation Acts cut the Dutch out of English trade with her colonies and with the Baltic, by 1689 English shipping in these areas trebled. The number of English seamen increased with equal rapidity, providing a vital strategic resource for war fighting, and ending the Dutch superiority in seafaring skills. However, the gradual waning of Dutch maritime power was primarily caused by the long and costly land wars with France after 1671. The French attacks forced the Dutch to become a major military power, and to seek allies, notably the English. To secure English support the Dutch had to make commercial concessions. Consequently the English, despite the relative failure of the Second and Third Dutch Wars, profited from the opportunities they created. Although the Dutch maritime economy remained strong for another century, it never recovered the naval power that had defied England and France combined in 1673. Protectionist legislation, strategic advantage and military distraction enabled the English to weaken Dutch mercantile dominance, laying the foundation for their own maritime power.

In this process the development of the specialist battle fleet was critical. Even allowing for the close proximity of the protagonists, and the importance of the issues at stake, the frequency of battles was astonishing. In 1673 there were three full-scale battles, in 1666 five full days of main fleet fighting. It is little wonder that the line of battle developed so quickly. The concentrated power of broadside-armed ships enabled the English to take the initiative at sea, using their superior position and defensive tactics to threaten the Dutch economy, the core of Dutch existence. That the English could not inflict a decisive defeat demonstrates the resilience of the Dutch economy, the weakness of English finances, the limits of the linear battle and the masterful performance of de Ruyter.

CHAPTER THREE

The Rise and Fall of the French Navy 1680–1713

The bonfire of ambition. Defeated in battle and without a safe Channel harbour, Louis XIV's battle fleet was destroyed by English boats and fireships at La Hougue, 22 May 1692. The ships were actually broadside on to the sea, and stripped of their sails. The largest ship is Le Soleil Royal, *the fleet flagship, named for the king. (Adriaen Van Diest)*

The Rise and Fall of the French Navy 1680–1713

B Y THE END OF the Third Anglo-Dutch War France possessed the world's largest battle fleet. France, the most powerful European state, had a population twice that of England, and ten times that of the Dutch Republic, which provided a massive tax yield to fuel the ambitions of her king, Louis XIV (1643–1715), who wanted to expand the land frontiers of France.

Louis's Minister of Finance, the Marine, Colonies and Trade, Jean Baptiste Colbert (1619–83), favoured a maritime empire. Although he indulged Colbert, Louis was more interested in Spain, and attacking the Protestant Dutch Republic, than advancing the interests of French merchants. France did not depend on overseas commerce, so a navy was useful, but hardly vital. Louis was simply not interested in the navy, and this proved critical, for when forced to choose between military and naval forces, he would always favour the army. The problem was exacerbated by the separate Mediterranean and Atlantic fleets. The French Navy never secured that place in the national, as opposed to regional, consciousness that gave the Dutch and English navies their strength. The interest groups representing commerce and colonies were simply too small to sustain Colbert's vision, while his king would always compromise on maritime issues if he could secure a fortress. England and the Netherlands, however, relied on the sea and responded to adversity with increased naval activity.

The French naval revival began in the 1650s, and by the mid 1670s Colbert had created a fleet, infrastructure, administration, bureaucracy and industrial base to outstrip England and Holland. Colbert also attacked Dutch commerce, using punitive tariffs to drive them out of French trade. Yet the French fleet was not built to attack Holland or England. Crucially, France did not develop a deep water harbour in the Channel. While Dunkirk was a formidable cruiser station, it could never support a battle fleet. Possibly Colbert anticipated acquiring Antwerp and the Scheldt Estuary, relying on his master's continental ambitions to complete the French naval position. Instead, the main base development of Louis's reign took place at Rochefort, on the Atlantic coast, linked by the Canal du Midi to the Mediterranean. This reflected Louis's ambitions. Uninterested in commerce, his ultimate aim was to secure the throne of Spain for his family. A fleet to cut Spain off from the Spanish Netherlands and her Atlantic empire, which could also exclude the maritime powers from the Mediterranean, would be a key instrument. Louis encouraged the maritime powers to fight each other and patronized the restored Stuarts to secure control of the English fleet. However, increasing suspicion of French continental ambitions took England out of the war in 1674 and into alliance with the Dutch. Arguing with the Dutch over trade seemed a trifle petty when France was on the verge of continental hegemony.

Between 1665 and 1670 Colbert carried out the largest shipbuilding programme yet seen in western Europe. He built sixty-five battleships, taking France ahead of the combined fleets of England and Holland. Among them were ten three-deckers, the largest ships afloat. For the next twenty years the French had a battle fleet of 120–140,000 tons. The Dutch never matched these figures, and England did so only after 1690. However, manning and using this impressive fleet was more difficult than building it. French naval performances before 1690 were rarely better than adequate, reflecting the length of time it took to produce experienced sea-officers and trained personnel. Only hard-won sea experience could bring the French up to the front rank of naval powers.

The Dutch war of 1672–8 exposed the dilemma of French policy. Colbert wanted to supplant the Dutch in world trade; Louis wanted the Spanish Netherlands. The threat posed by these policies to the stability of Europe and the interests of the other major powers turned the Dutch struggle into a European war. After England left the war in 1674, the French did not attack the Dutch in the Channel. Instead Louis, revealing his true interests, sent his fleet to attack Spain. A small Dutch fleet under de Ruyter went to assist the Spanish, but de Ruyter was defeated and died of his wounds off Sicily in April 1676. Dutch seapower would never recover: it lacked the resources to match the ever larger fleets of France and England, while William of Orange was forced to sacrifice Dutch naval and maritime interests to support the land war. Unable to crush the Dutch, however, Louis made peace. The Treaty of Nymegen of 1678 restored Dutch territory and, significantly, cut many of Colbert's anti-Dutch tariffs. The French challenge had also produced a powerful reaction in London. The English 1677 programme provided thirty new battleships, including ten three-deckers. These ships demonstrated that the Stuart state had the political will to resist France.

In 1685 Louis revoked the Edict of Nantes, which had given religious tolerance to the Protestant Huguenots. The subsequent exodus of artisans, merchants, seafarers, soldiers and administrators – some 200,000 people – to Holland, England, Sweden and the Protestant German states, weakened France and was a particularly serious blow to the maritime sector. Furthermore, Colbert's influence over the king had been waning for some time before his death in 1683. His son, the Marquis de Seignelay, succeeded to his portfolio, but died in 1690. Thereafter, the French Navy continued to lose influence and power. Seignelay had begun a major expansion in 1690, taking the fleet to 190,000 tons by 1695, but this was a brief, unrepresentative figure. By 1715 the fleet stood at no more than 100,000 tons, a figure that would fall by half within another five years. France could not afford to have both a fleet on this scale and the largest army in Europe. By raising the stakes for command of the sea after 1690 with an arms race, the English defeated the French challenge, but they did so in the legislature, rather than at sea.

The war of the League of Augsburg (1688–97) demonstrated both the success of Colbert's policy and the fragility of his navy. For all the 'naval' power it could mobilize in 1690, the French state lacked the maritime strength in depth for a long war. France simply could not mobilize the manpower and maritime resources to keep this force effective. In September 1688 Louis invaded the Rhineland, which enabled William of Orange to invade England and overthrow the unpopular Catholic regime of his father-in-law, James II. This ruined Louis's plans, which had relied on William and James neutralizing each other while he dealt with the German states. Consequently, the French reaction to William's move was slow and ill co-ordinated. The French sent troops and supplies to Ireland to support James, but after the drawn battle of Bantry Bay in 1689 they lost local naval superiority, enabling William, now King William III, to defeat James at the Boyne in July 1690. This was a critical victory, as the Anglo-Dutch alliance had just lost a major sea battle.

In 1690 both the English and the Dutch had been slow to mobilize their fleets, enabling the French to combine their Atlantic and Mediterranean fleets at Brest under Vice Admiral Anne Hilarion de Cotentin, Comte de Tourville (1642–1701), perhaps the greatest French admiral. Tourville was ordered to destroy the allied fleet. He had seventy ships to meet the allies' fifty-seven, and an even greater firepower superiority. The allied commander, Arthur Herbert, Earl of Torrington, recognized that defeat would be disastrous for the new regime and skilfully avoided battle. He knew that while he had a 'fleet in being' the French would not try to invade. Unfortunately, Torrington's enemies persuaded Queen Mary that he was being unduly cautious and the Crown Council William had left to advise her during his absence in Ireland ordered him to give battle.

The fleets finally engaged off Beachy Head on 10 July 1690. Under the circumstances Torrington's attempt to fight a partial battle, enough to satisfy those at a distance, without taking undue risks, was logical. But the Dutch van squadron ignored its orders and launched a furious assault on the French. While the English rear squadron had the advantage over its opposite number, Tourville used his numerical superiority to double on the head and rear of the Dutch, while in the centre Torrington fought a holding action. In the evening the wind died and Torrington ordered his fleet to anchor without taking in sail, outwitting Tourville, whose fleet

*A contemporary view of the battle of Beachy Head, giving the old-style date of
30 June 1690, following the Julian calendar then in use in England. The view
emphasizes the different tactics adopted by the three allied squadrons.*

drifted past. Remarkably only one Dutch ship was captured, when,
having lost her anchors, she drifted into the French line. When Torrington
tried to escape past the French to the Thames, to deter an invasion, ten
more allied ships were taken or burnt, all but one from the crippled
Dutch squadron. Although it was the odds that had defeated Torrington,
he was made a scapegoat to save the alliance with the Dutch. However,
his 'fleet in being' became a key concept in naval thought, and his tactical
ideas became the core of new *Fighting Instructions*. Both the English and
French introduced permanent flag signal codes in 1693 to convey an
admiral's instructions to his fleet. While the system remained limited, and
almost impossible to use once the firing started, it was an advance on
sending messages by boat.

For all the glory of Beachy Head, Tourville's victory was singularly
devoid of strategic impact, as the French were not ready to invade.
After burning a fishing village, Tourville had to put back to Brest, his

The wind being. N.N.W.

The line of y͛ french fleet standing. N.N.W.

The

English

Chanel

W

S N

a Scale of 12 English milles

The Beachy
or
Cap Beucher

Part of England

admiral calemburg of amsterdam
English ships of y͛ red flagg who
...gag'd w͛ y͛ french
...utch fire schips
...s set on fire
D, c, were sunckt

A.A. The french fleet of 76, capital schips on
a line from y͛ S,S,E, to y͛ N.N.W.
B. 3 other capital ships
C. 4 galless : D, 2 how't E, 31 fire ships
F. fregatts and tenders.
Divition 1 y͛ vinguard, 1, a rear admiral
2, vice admiral m͛ damfroville with y͛ bleu and
white flagg. 3 .a Cornett

The main body 4, vice admiral m͛ Tourville
with y͛ white flagg
5.a rear admiral, 6, a Cornett
y͛ rear. 7, a panfront
8 vice admirll Chateaurenauld with the
bleu flagg.
9. a rear admiral.

crews decimated by sickness. More important objectives, like supporting James's army, were impossible to achieve: the endurance of fleets at this time was determined more by the deterioration of food and water, and the rapid spread of disease, than the weather. Here the French invariably suffered more than the allies, with the insanitary state of their ships reflecting their limited sea experience. In 1691 Tourville, now heavily outnumbered by a revitalized allied fleet, switched his attention to allied convoys.

In 1692 the French finally assembled an army to invade England. Louis believed a battle would clear the path for an invasion, and expected some English officers would desert to the Stuart cause. Tourville, like Torrington in 1690, was ordered, against his better judgement, to engage a superior enemy. As the Toulon squadron failed to reach Brest in time, and he was also short of seamen, Tourville entered the Channel with only forty-four ships.

Sighting Admiral Sir Edward Russell's allied fleet of eighty-eight ships off Cape Barfleur on 29 May 1692, Tourville accepted his fate and directed his flagship, *Le Soleil Royal*, to engage Russell's HMS

Britannia. The two great three-deckers became the core of the battle, with other ships drifting in and out of their duel. After ten hours the wind increased and Tourville disengaged. Although his flagship had been rendered almost unmanageable by her English opponent, his fleet remained united. The next morning Russell sighted the French, by now somewhat reduced by ships breaking off for Brest, and ordered a pursuit. That night twenty French ships ran through the treacherous Alderney race to safety, but fifteen remained on the Normandy coast. Three were aground at Cherbourg and twelve close inshore at La Hougue, where the French invasion army had assembled. On 2 June, with James II watching, Admiral Rooke led a boat attack that destroyed the French ships, most of which were three-deckers of the heaviest class. The ex-king had the mortifying experience of watching a fleet that he more than anyone had helped to build, destroy his last

The gratitude of a nation. After Barfleur/La Hougue a grateful Queen Mary decided that the Royal Palace at Greenwich should be completed as a hospital for disabled seamen. No finer tribute has ever been paid to the lower deck personnel of any navy. The buildings remain among the finest architectural compositions ever executed. (Antonio Canaletto)

hope for restoration. It was entirely in character, however, that he cheered the English seamen.

The suffering of the wounded persuaded Queen Mary to convert the incomplete Royal Palace at Greenwich into a naval hospital and long-term accommodation for disabled and elderly seamen. It remains to this day the finest tribute ever paid by a grateful nation to its sailors.

The loss of fifteen ships at La Hougue was a serious blow to French prestige, particularly when so many of them were named for the king, but they were replaced with ease. Between 1691 and 1692 France launched almost 100,000 tons of battleships, and by 1695 the French fleet was even larger than it had been in 1690 (190,000 tons compared to 122,000 tons). Yet the fleet was never used. After a famine and a financial crisis in 1693–4 France had to concentrate her resources on the army. Furthermore, she had neither the men nor the equipment to put the ships to sea. A close allied blockade denied her access to Baltic naval stores and Swedish cannon. The French had been short of 2,000 cannon when the war broke out, and were never able to catch up. Once the invasion of England had been abandoned there was no worthwhile role for a battle fleet. In 1695 Marshal Vauban advised shifting to an attritional strategy, attacking allied commerce with naval squadrons and privateers. The privateering effort involved the loan of state warships, and mobilized a peculiarly economical form of maritime power. In 1693 Tourville's fleet had located the annual Levant and Mediterranean trade, the Smyrna convoy, off Cape St Vincent, defeated the escort and taken eighty ships. While this was disaster for the allies, it did not affect their ability to continue the war. Sea denial strategies are necessarily inconclusive, unless they can be converted into sea control. This was simply beyond the power of France, now that England had finally put in place the financial and political structures necessary to harness her own strategic potential.

Beachy Head had been a formative experience for the English. It reminded the political élite just how deeply they were committed to the 1688 Revolution. The threat of a Stuart restoration opened the national coffers, and Parliament agreed to rebuild the navy. Twenty-seven new battleships were laid down. In 1693–4 the ability of the English state to finance war was revolutionized by the creation of the English National Debt and the Bank of England. The National Debt transformed the old, short-term royal debt, which had been the Achilles' heel of the Royal Navy in the Second and Third Dutch wars, into a long-term investment in the State, while the Bank would organize and regulate the state's finances. The two measures provided the long-term financial strength that underpinned the rise of Britain from an offshore island to a global empire. Their impact was immediate: in its first year the Bank effectively paid for the navy, restoring its credit with merchants and creating the basis for long-term naval finance. These financial innovations also tied the political and commercial élite to the Revolution settlement; Admiral Russell, victor of Barfleur and a leading politician, was among the largest investors in the Bank, for example. Only a disaffected minority now stood to gain from the restoration of the Stuarts; the men of power and property were committed to the new regime. This process provided the funds for further naval construction, and the development of a new base at Plymouth to support an Atlantic war. Having secured command of the sea and imposed a blockade, William III recognized that he must avoid defeat on land if he was to wear down the French. To this end he shifted English and, especially, Dutch resources to the land war.

As the French had abandoned the contest for the Channel, William III widened his attack on the French economy by sending the allied fleet into the Mediterranean in 1694, where it supported the Spanish against the French, and kept it there over the winter. This distant service exposed the limitations of existing English battleships. Having been designed for short-range, high-tempo combat in the Channel, they were too small to carry the provisions, spare gear, stores and ammunition for long periods away from their bases. New and bigger ships were required to make seapower effective at a distance.

After 1694, the French *guerre de course* was essentially conducted by privateers and hired warships run for profit, and it imposed huge demands on the allies. They blockaded and bombarded the privateer bases at Dunkirk, St Malo and Calais, used convoys, and developed sophisticated insurance markets to spread the financial risk. The failure of the French to use their battle fleet after 1694 led the Admiralty to give convoy escorts and cruisers priority over the Grand Fleet. What little glory there was in this kind of petty war went to the privateers, among whom the Dunkirker Jean Bart, exemplar of an old local tradition, achieved mythic status. Privateering kept the French maritime sector involved in the war without costing the state any money. However, it failed to break the allied dominance of maritime trade, which funded their long war with France. Allied endurance negated French victories on land.

There was a brief truce after the Peace of Ryswick in 1697, only for the struggle to resume in 1702, for a bigger prize. In the War of the

Spanish Succession (1702–14) England (later Britain, after the 1707 Act of Union with Scotland), Holland, and the Holy Roman Empire denied the throne of an undivided Spanish empire to Louis XIV's grandson. The war at sea was one-sided: France could not contest the English Channel with the allies, and after 1704 abandoned the Mediterranean. The destruction of a Franco-Spanish fleet at Vigo in 1702 prevented French access to the treasure of Spanish America. When an allied amphibious attack captured Gibraltar on 24 July 1704, the French committed their main fleet. The Comte de Toulouse, a 26-year-old royal bastard, took fifty-one ships to meet Admiral Rooke with a similar allied force. As the allies were short of ammunition and men, Rooke, despite having the weather gauge, had to fight a defensive battle. When the fleets met off Malaga on 24 August, Toulouse tried to break through the allied line to exploit his superior firepower. Skilful

ship and squadron handling by the commander of the van squadron, Sir Cloudesley Shovell (1659–1707), thwarted his move, then relieved Rooke's hard-pressed centre division. At nightfall Toulouse broke off the action, unaware that the allies were almost out of ammunition. The strategic victory went to the allies. Thereafter English naval power dominated the Mediterranean.

One of the greatest admirals of the age. Sir Cloudesley Shovell (1659–1707), an outstanding seaman, had been raised in the service by fellow Norfolk-born officers. He proved himself at every level, including service against Algerine corsairs, as a junior admiral at Barfleur and Malaga, and as a fleet commander worked harmoniously with the army and his allies, notably at the capture of Barcelona. (Michael Dahl)

The lure of treasure. An Anglo-Dutch fleet under Admiral Rooke stormed into the harbour of Vigo on the north coast of Spain on 13 October 1702. After breaking the defensive boom the allies overwhelmed the defences and captured eleven Spanish silver galleons and ten French battleships. The treasure was destined for the French war effort, and its loss was a bitter blow to Louis XIV. The battle saved Rooke's reputation, and career, after a failure before Cádiz. Treasure hunters continue to search for the silver, although it was almost all accounted for at the time. Part was already ashore. Rooke took the rest.

Returning home late in the season Sir Cloudesley Shovell, the British Mediterranean commander, had the misfortune to run on to the Scilly Isles with part of his fleet. On 22 October 1707 his flagship, the three-decker *Association*, was wrecked. The admiral was murdered after he struggled ashore. (Some records assert that he was drowned.) This disaster, the result of navigational errors, prompted the search for a reliable method of determining longitude. In an age much given to public funerary monuments, Shovell was accorded a place of honour in the national pantheon, Westminster Abbey, his tomb crowned with a singularly inappropriate statue of a well-dressed grandee in a full wig. Born in north Norfolk, Shovell had risen through the ranks on ability,

and the patronage of his relatives. He was the very archetype of the fighting sea officers who gave Britain the advantage at sea. Like their Dutch predecessors, these men were bred to the sea, combining good sense with personal ambition.

After 1704 French naval activity was dominated by increasingly ambitious attacks on trade. Powerful privateer squadrons commanded by Chevalier Forbin and René Duguay-Trouin attacked convoys. Backed by the personal investment of the king, Duguay hired a battle squadron in 1712, which he used to capture and ransom Rio de Janeiro. This profound change in French naval policy from fleet battle to oceanic warfare was reflected in a shift from three-decked battleships to

big two-decked ships. France had abandoned her attempt to secure command of the sea. Aside from a few morale-boosting victories, the great battle fleet of Colbert had achieved surprisingly little. With the Dutch declining into a second-class navy configured to defend trade and colonies, Britain became dominant at sea. The Treaty of Utrecht confirmed her possession of Gibraltar and Minorca, the keys to the Mediterranean, and paved the way for further conflict in the Americas by securing Newfoundland and Nova Scotia.

While England, Holland and France fought over the Atlantic and the Mediterranean, developments in the Baltic facilitated the expansion of oceanic naval power into the northern sea.

Returning late in the year Shovell's squadron misjudged their longitude. His flagship, HMS Association, *with others, ran on to the Scilly Isles. This led the Government to offer a reward for a reliable method of determining longitude, resulting in John Harrison's chronometer.*

CHAPTER FOUR

The Baltic in the Eighteenth Century: Seapower in an Inland Sea

*King Gustavus III directs his inshore
galley fleet at the battle at Frederickshamn,
15 May 1790, from the Royal Yacht* Amphion.
*His attack on the Russian flotilla failed,
and the Swedes were driven back to
Svensksund. Because this type of combat
was slower-paced and less fluid than battle
under sail, it tended to favour the big
battalions. (Johan Tietrich Schoultz)*

The Baltic in the Eighteenth Century: Seapower in an Inland Sea

THE GREAT NORTHERN WAR 1700–21

Throughout the second half of the seventeenth century Sweden dominated the Baltic region, her empire based on sea control. In February 1700 a makeshift alliance of Denmark, Russia and Saxony/Poland (two separate states but both ruled by Augustus II, hereditary King of Saxony and elected King of Poland) attacked Sweden in Holstein, Livonia, Ingria and Estonia, hoping to exploit the youth and inexperience of the 18-year-old king, Charles XII. Concerned that Denmark might take control of the Sound and Belts at the entrance to the Baltic, and exclude their shipping, Britain and Holland provided Sweden with naval support. Charles seized the initiative in July, crossing the Sound to attack Copenhagen and drive Denmark out of the war. As Denmark was the only one of the allies with a fleet, this success gave Charles complete control of the Baltic, which he promptly employed to ship his army to Ingria, where he destroyed the Russian army at Narva. In a single season the young king had demonstrated the advantages of a central position, allied to complete control of sea communications. However, Charles did not pay

BATTLES IN THE BALTIC
The Baltic witnessed the most remarkable strategic transformation during the Great Northern war, 1700–21, when the Swedish Empire, which controlled almost the entire coastline from north Germany, through Poland, Finland and Sweden, lost control of the entire southern coast. The key to this shift was the loss of sea control, without which the small Swedish Army could not be moved to meet each new threat. Thereafter the region witnessed little change before 1809.

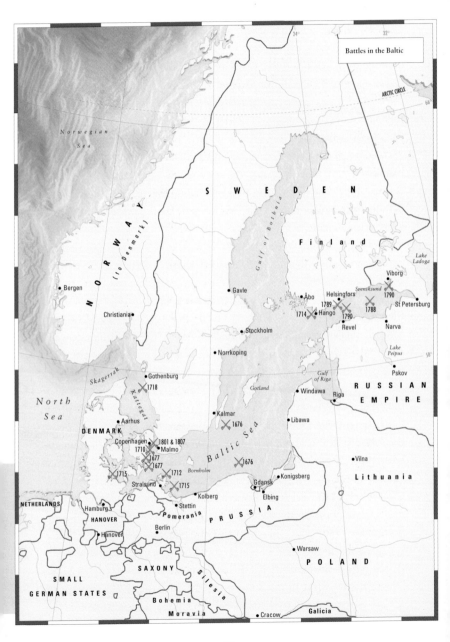

sufficient attention to his naval position. By contrast the Russian tsar, Peter the Great, secured access to the Baltic at St Petersburg in 1702, and began to build a fleet. The Swedes gradually lost control of the upper reaches of the Gulf of Finland.

After crushing Saxony and taking control of Poland, Charles finally turned to deal with Russia. Underrating his enemy after the easy success of Narva, and lured on by promises of local support, Charles allowed his army to be drawn deep into the Ukraine where, his troops exhausted and their supply lines cut, he was decisively defeated at Poltava in 1709. The folly of abandoning his secure Baltic base demonstrated the limits of Charles's strategic vision. It is doubtful if his army, with a secure maritime supply line, would have been defeated.

Denmark rejoined the war after Poltava. Her fleet immediately complicated the movement of Swedish troops, ruining the Swedish position on the southern shores of the Baltic. After an indecisive battle in 1710, the Danes crippled a big military convoy to the Pomeranian fortress of Stralsund in 1712. With the bulk of her navy deployed against the Danes, Swedish forces in the Gulf of Finland were outnumbered by the Russians, and on 6 August 1714 one hundred Russian galleys overpowered seven Swedish sailing warships at Hango after a prolonged and costly battle. The following year the Danish fleet blockading Stralsund defeated the Swedish fleet, enabling an allied amphibious force to capture a key offshore position, sealing the fate of the fortress. These operations were supported by a British fleet which had entered the Baltic with the Dutch to protect their commerce against Swedish privateers. The new king of Britain, George I, was also Elector of Hanover, and his continental ambitions gave a new importance to the Baltic. Charles had hoped the privateers would deny Russia any economic benefit from the recently conquered Baltic provinces, but Britain and Holland would not allow the supply of naval stores to be interrupted. In 1716 Danish warships destroyed the Swedish galley fleet in the Sound, crippling Charles XII's attempt to invade Norway. In 1719 Russian galleys landed troops to ravage the

Stockholm region and, after Charles XII's death, a Danish amphibious force bombarded and captured the Swedish fleet and base at Marstrand, wiping out Swedish communications for operations in Norway. The same year Britain made peace with Sweden, and tried to remove Russian influence from north Germany in order to re-establish a Baltic balance. The former policy was successful, but the latter proved impossible. Sweden was now too weak and isolated to return to the front rank of European states. However, a British battle fleet and the Swedish galleys were able to restrict Russian naval activity between 1719 and 1721, when the Peace of Nystad ended the war.

The combat at Hango, 6 August 1714, occurred at a critical strategic point, where the difficult inshore navigation, suitable only for galleys, could be interrupted by deep-draught sailing ships. The victory of the Russian galleys paved the way for a series of amphibious raids on the Swedish coast. (Alexei Zubov)

The collapse of the Swedish Empire was the result of naval attrition. Sweden simply did not have the naval power to deal with the fleets of Denmark and Russia operating at opposite ends of the Baltic, and so her naval forces, adequate against either, were whittled down in small-scale, largely indecisive actions. These minor defeats culminated in the loss of Stralsund and the ravaging of the Swedish coast. The process was hastened by the loss of vital commercial revenues. Unable to use the sea, Sweden could not move her army to meet the allied attacks.

Until 1725 the combination of Russia's Baltic ambitions with a dramatic naval build-up was seen as a challenge by the British. The new Russian Navy proved to be short-lived, for although it acquired many ships, the majority were second-hand Indiamen and heavy cruisers, sold off at the end of the Spanish war. Peter's fleet was incapable of meeting a regular battle fleet in open water. In 1723, after Peter's death, the Russian Navy collapsed and did not recover for over half a century. With Sweden diminished, Denmark weakened and Russia resuming her old land orientation, the Baltic remained open to the dominant European navy.

The Baltic remained a critical source of naval supplies throughout the next century, but only once did the regional powers fight for control of the sea.

RUSSIA, TURKEY AND SWEDEN 1768–95

Navies have always projected power ashore, attacking ports, harbours, and coastal towns. By 1760 the British were the masters of amphibious warfare, conducting large-scale operations against France and Spain. However, the major players in littoral warfare, the combined operations of land and sea forces, were the Russians. From Peter the Great's time, Russian seapower had been dominated by an expansive state policy to acquire land from her neighbours, Turkey and Sweden. While it remained littoral in character, and was only used against weaker states, Russian seapower was a powerful instrument. But when Russia tried to join the front rank of naval powers she discovered that oceanic seapower, unlike littoral strength, could not be extemporized in wartime.

In 1768 Russia and Turkey went to war, and the following year the Russians sent part of their Baltic fleet into the Mediterranean. The arrival of the fleet reflected significant British support, ranging from dockyard work to the presence of numerous Scottish officers. When the Russians located the Turkish fleet off Izmir in July 1770, they drove them into the bay of Chesmé and destroyed them with a fireship attack the following night. This ancient tactic worked in a crowded anchorage against ill-disciplined opponents, but the fleet did not have any direct influence on the war. Without an army to exploit their success, the Russians could only harass the coast of Asia Minor and Greece, and the Turks could always bring up enough troops to deny them a foothold ashore. The peace signed in 1774 gave Russia a foothold on the Black Sea, and in 1783 they annexed the Crimea, including the great natural harbour of Sevastopol, which dominated the theatre. Turkey declared war in 1787, but by 1788 the Russians had captured Ochakov,

The strategic flexibility of naval force enabled the Russian Baltic fleet, with British support, to operate in the eastern Mediterranean. Consequently the Russians could attack Turkey in the Black Sea and the Aegean. At Chesmé a badly handled Turkish fleet, driven into a cul-de-sac, was destroyed by fireships.

key to the River Bug and the Ukraine. They followed up their success by securing control of the River Dnieper in a battle on 28–29 June, involving troops, forts, galleys and sailing ships. In the following year their flotilla entered the Danube. At sea the Russians gradually took control from the more numerous, but badly handled Turkish fleet. More significantly, the Russians began to rely on native officers, mercenaries like the American John Paul Jones being replaced by men like Admiral Ushakov. In the Black Sea, Russian seapower made an important contribution to success on land, providing fire support, amphibious power projection and logistics. Peace was signed in 1792, leaving Russia dominant in the Black Sea, and in possession of the important harbour at Odessa.

The Turkish war provided the Swedish King Gustavus III with an opportunity to recover Finnish territory lost to Russia in the 1740s. In 1788 Gustavus launched a maritime campaign in the Gulf of Finland, hoping to exploit the relative weakness of the Russians to attack Cronstadt and St Petersburg. With his army crippled by political factions, Gustavus's hopes rested on the navy and the new inshore fleet based at the fortress arsenal of Sweaborg. However, the Russian battle fleet blocked the Swedish advance at Hogland in 1788. In 1789 and 1790, relying on superior numbers, the Russians gradually weakened the Swedes, until by mid 1790 they had trapped the Swedish battle fleet in the Bay of Viborg. Here Gustavus III took command of the inshore flotilla and lead a full-scale breakout on 3 July. Despite the loss of several battleships and other vessels, the Swedes broke open the Russian position, inflicting heavy losses. In 1790 the Swedes lost ten battleships, five of which were added to the Russian fleet.

The final battle of the war, at Svensksund on 9–10 July 1790, was a coastal struggle between 195 Swedish coastal warships and 140 Russian units. The Russians had a significant advantage in men and guns. The Swedes were anchored in a defensive position between islands in a strong L-shaped formation. On the first day the Russian flotilla attacked from the south, but was scattered by the wind and sea, and heavily damaged by the fire of the Swedish coastal forces, including positions ashore, anchored galley frigates and gunboats. The Swedish gunboats then advanced their left flank, enfilading the Russian line. As the Russian gunboats retreated their galleys were overcome by the sea, or driven ashore, while some of the sailing ships, unable to move, were boarded, captured or burnt. The action ended at 10 p.m. At daybreak the next morning the Swedes followed up their success with a full-scale attack on the Russians, who broke and fled. Over the two days the Russians lost 7,500 dead, wounded or captured and 64 vessels sunk or taken. The Swedes suffered 300 casualties, and lost four vessels.

Svensksund was a triumph for new coastal warfare ideas, emphasizing firepower over mobility, and the resolve of the Swedes. However, the battle could not make up for the heavy losses of the sailing fleet, which was now little more than half the strength of the Russian fleet. Consequently, the victory could only stabilize the Swedish land/sea front, while Catherine II, anxious to settle one of the two wars that Russia was fighting, accepted the *status quo ante*.

Littoral warfare, which combined sailing ships, oared craft and troops, could be highly effective, but only if the problems of command and co-ordination created by operating in three distinct elements were resolved, and communication systems developed to control such diverse forces. The Swedish breakout from Viborg and their victory at Svensksund reflected good planning, limited spread of forces and the co-ordinating presence of the king. The Russians, with long experience of such operations, usually gave the military commander supreme authority over the naval forces. In the Black Sea they developed considerable skill, relative to the Turks, but in the Baltic their coastal warships proved to be outmoded, and their commanders unimaginative. The ultimate development of coastal warfare in the age of sail would have to wait until new circumstances reconfigured the Royal Navy as a power-projection force.

CHAPTER FIVE

The Dawn of Global Conflict 1739–63

*For those in peril on the sea. The French 74
Thesée founders after opening her lower deck
gunports during the battle of Quiberon Bay,
20 November 1759. Only twenty of her crew
survived. Despite the heavy weather that day
her captain had attempted to use his lower
deck guns and paid the ultimate price. That
afternoon the French lost both the battle and
the war for global empire. (Richard Paton)*

The Dawn of Global Conflict 1739–63

B Y 1713 BRITAIN WAS the strongest seapower, but her power was restricted to the European theatre, as a disastrous attack on Quebec in 1711 had demonstrated. Outside Europe, systematic operations were still unusual and raiding the norm. Over the next fifty years Britain developed the overseas bases, reliable logistics, more durable ships, increased reserves of manpower, improved health and techniques of amphibious warfare required for global power.

After 1713 Britain used her economic strength to maintain the Royal Navy at a very high level; by 1730 it was equal in size to the next three or four navies. The fleet supported the more 'continental' diplomacy of the new Hanoverian Dynasty, which was often accused of placing German interests above British. Britain certainly acquired considerable influence in Europe, particularly during a post-war alliance with France that lasted into the 1730s. Naval power opened the way for trade. Britain had exploited the War of the Spanish Succession to secure a dominant interest in Portuguese commerce, in return for naval and diplomatic protection, a type of indirect empire preferable to regular colonies. It was a model British merchants hoped to impose on Spain.

The Mediterranean ambitions of the Spanish king, Philip V, soon brought him into conflict with Britain. When Spain invaded Sicily, Admiral Sir George Byng destroyed her fleet off Cape Passaro on 11 August 1718. The Spanish tried to escape but Byng abandoned the line, ordering a 'general chase'. His ships engaged the enemy as they came up, leaving disabled ships to be taken by those following. Cape Passaro ended Spain's Italian ambitions for a decade. Byng's 'pursuit battle' would become a critical tactic, but only when well-manned fleets commanded by admirals with significant practical experience were available. After the war ended in 1720 the Spanish Navy was rebuilt as a cruiser fleet for the Mediterranean and Atlantic.

The collapse of the French Navy after 1713 reflected weak finances and the restricted horizons of the old king and the regent for his 5-year-old successor. Although French commercial interests benefited from privileged access to the Spanish market, and the success of their West Indian colonies, the navy was moribund. Without money or a role, the French Navy, dominated by the internal politics of the Court, ossified. While naval doctrine favoured a fleet of two-decked ships to avoid close combat, the few new ships actually built were generally under-armed and too lightly constructed for sustained sea service. The one innovation of the period was the frigate, a single-decked ship designed for commercial raiding and scouting, with an emphasis on speed. French frigates proved too fast for British two-decked cruisers and small battleships, forcing the British to build their own frigates. However, when France next went to war she would find her fleet a broken reed.

The close links between France and Spain created by the Bourbon 'Family Compact' of 1733 might have challenged the British in time, but the Bourbon fleets lacked firepower and close-quarters fighting strength. Their doctrine, which favoured extended operations in support of commerce and colonial conquests, was checkmated by heavily built, durable and powerfully armed British three-decked ships, which reflected the 'decisive battle' doctrine of the Royal Navy. The Bourbon navies could hamper British use of the sea, but they could not exert control.

THE WAR OF JENKINS'S EAR

Spanish commercial interests in the West Indies were defended against illegal British traders by local *guarda-costas* (coast-guard units charged with preventing foreign trade with the Spanish islands and mainland). Their violent methods reflected royal policy and the self-financing nature of their operation. During a scuffle aboard a British merchant ship off Cuba in 1731, a *guarda-costa* officer cut off one of Captain Robert Jenkins's ears. When the pickled appendage was produced in the House of Commons in 1738 it became the focus for political

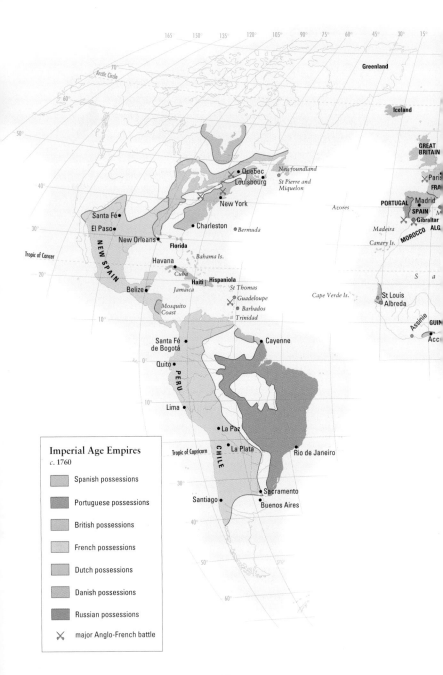

Arctic Circle

Greenland

Iceland

GREAT
BRITAIN

Quebec   Newfoundland   Paris
Louisbourg   St Pierre and   FRA
                Miquelon
     New York

                                  Azores   PORTUGAL Madrid
Santa Fé   SPAIN
El Paso   Gibraltar
     New Orleans   Charleston   Bermuda   Madeira   ALG
                                                                              MOROCCO
                  Florida   Canary Is.

NEW SPAIN   Bahama Is.   S   a

          Havana
                Cuba   Hispaniola
          Jamaica   Haiti   St Thomas   Cape Verde Is.   St Louis
     Belize   Guadeloupe   Albreda
          Mosquito   Barbados   Assinie
          Coast   Trinidad   GUIN
                                                                                     Acc

                        Santa Fé   Cayenne
                        de Bogotá
                   Quito

              PERU

          Lima

                   La Paz
                        La Plata
Tropic of Capricorn   CHILE   Rio de Janeiro

Santiago   Sacramento
                    Buenos Aires

Imperial Age Empires
c. 1760

- Spanish possessions

- Portuguese possessions

- British possessions

- French possessions

- Dutch possessions

- Danish possessions

- Russian possessions

✕   major Anglo-French battle

EMPIRES IN THE IMPERIAL AGE, c. 1760

A new field for naval enterprise. By the mid eighteenth century war between the great commercial powers was not only about global empire, it was also waged around the world by increasingly effective, durable and flexible fleets, staging through chains of bases, and reliant on local infrastructure.

pressure demanding war. The merchant community wanted the Royal Navy to secure them fresh commercial privileges. Having paid for an overwhelmingly powerful navy for twenty-five years, the merchants demanded a reasonable return on their investment. Their ambitions were reflected in British strategy, blockading Spanish ports, attacking trade and seizing colonies.

The war was launched in the Caribbean in 1739 with the capture of Porto Bello on the South American mainland by Admiral Edward Vernon (1684–1757). However, this proved to be a false dawn. A larger amphibious force sent to the theatre in 1740 failed at Cartagena, defeated by inter-service quarrels, stout Spanish resistance, uncertainty about the French response and the inevitable ravages of West Indian disease. By the close of the season 10,000 men had died. In this theatre the defences built by Philip II combined with disease to stave off British maritime power for another generation. The experience of 1740–48 proved a vital stepping-stone to the amphibious triumphs of 1756–63. In most other respects the war proved to be equally disappointing, the treasure fleets and easy victories anticipated in London failing to materialize.

The War of Jenkins's Ear demonstrated that the instruments of seapower would have to be improved before they could be used to full effect so far from home. Caribbean warfare was governed by disease and lack of manpower. Men arrived in the West Indies after an Atlantic crossing weakened by scurvy, the wasting disease caused by lack of vitamin C. When sent ashore to the 'hospitals' they were exposed to yellow fever, the fatal mosquito-borne disease. Up to 15 per cent of the crews of newly arrived ships would be killed by this lethal combination. Thereafter, the losses among men inured to the area were relatively light, but that still left the fleet to find replacements, which were always in short supply. Desertion only added to the problem. The British bases on Jamaica and Antigua relied on the American colonies for food and timber, while naval stores and medicine came from Britain. To support Vernon's fleet the local bases had to be developed, manned and supplied. As few men volunteered to serve in the West

Indies, the development of naval bases proved to be a costly and complex task for naval administration. Almost all supplies had to be sent out to meet anticipated demands, and it was not until the 1740s that the British Admiralty was sufficiently well-established, and credit-worthy, to carry out this task. Despite the disasters of 1740, the fleet was never held up by lack of food, stores or gunpowder, which was a tremendous achievement.

The most ambitious British strategy of war did not rely on bases. A squadron was sent to attack Spain in the Pacific under Commodore George Anson (1697–1762). Setting out in 1740, Anson's squadron was dispersed by storms and decimated by scurvy by the time it entered the Pacific. It was a testament to Anson's indomitable will that it persevered and triumphed. HMS *Centurion* captured the annual silver galleon en route from Acapulco to Manila, and then Anson went on to complete the first British circumnavigation since Drake. The voyage and the treasure made Anson a national figure. Anson used his prize money to launch a political career, marrying the daughter of one of the most powerful men in the country, Lord Chancellor Hardwicke, and joining the Board of Admiralty. For the next eighteen years he dominated naval policy, improving every aspect of the service, from health care to tactics, by way of ship design and strategy. Anson ensured the Royal Navy overcame the deleterious effects of a thirty-year peace and the deadweight of custom and tradition. He improved the mobilization and treatment of naval manpower, developed the maritime component of British strategy and unified the officer corps around a common sense of professionalism that stood out against unwarranted political interference.

In European waters the Anglo-Spanish war was complicated by the coterminous War of the Austrian Succession, in which King George II took part only as the Elector of Hanover. Although France had planned to join Spain in a maritime war against Britain, an opportunistic shift of policy to exploit Prussian success against Austria deflected her back to Europe. Meanwhile, the British, based at Minorca, blockaded the

Spanish fleet in Toulon and cut her coastal trade. On 11 February 1744 the French and Spanish fleets left Toulon just before the French declared war on Britain. The battle of Toulon proved indecisive: the British commander, Matthews, failed to form a line, while his second, Lestock, refused to support him. While individual British officers fought well, notably Edward Hawke, the command failure wasted their superior fighting power. Under the linear *Fighting Instructions,* Lestock, the more culpable, escaped censure while Matthews was cashiered for failing to form a line.

Toulon was the only occasion the allies offered battle. They lacked the heavy ships to meet the Royal Navy: France had no three-decked ships, and Spain had only one. Instead, the French relied on privateers, not only to attack British trade, but also to carry the Young Pretender, Charles Edward Stuart, to Scotland in 1745. In a bizarre example of French court politics, the minister of marine refused to involve the navy in a potentially decisive strategy to overthrow the Hanoverian regime, because the Stuart cause was supported by his most bitter rival. He subcontracted the task to an Irish Jacobite privateer instead! British naval power denied Charles Edward Stuart much of the French force sent to help him, most of his gold, and all hope of worthwhile reinforcements.

In 1745 a Royal Navy force carried an colonial expedition to America to capture Louisbourg, the outer bastion of French Canada. The entire French position in the western hemisphere was crumbling for lack of contact with home. A large expedition sent out in 1746 collapsed under the strain of chaotic logistics, lack of money, weak leadership and typhus. It was a disaster of astonishing magnitude: thousands of sailors and soldiers died, ships were lost and the whole structure of the French Navy received a shattering blow. In India the French proved superior, winning a fleet action and securing the fall of Madras, although that was an isolated success.

In 1747 British numerical superiority, allied to superior financial resources, enabled Anson to deploy a strong battleship force in the Western Approaches (the sea area to the west of the English Channel

The second siege of Louisbourg in 1758, on Cape Breton off the Canadian coast. The French had invested heavily in this great fortress and base, but without command of the sea it was easily taken by a superior army. This success facilitated the attempt on Quebec the following season, which settled the war for North America.

and Atlantic coast of France, where north European shipping bound for the Americas or the Indies would necessarily pass). The 'Western Squadron' protected British shipping in this critical area, and intercepted French ships trying to leave European waters. On 3 May 1747 Anson, commanding seventeen battleships, annihilated five French battleships escorting a large French convoy bound for India and Canada off Cape Finisterre. On 14 October Rear Admiral Hawke's fourteen battleships captured nine French battleships escorting a West Indian convoy in the same area. These were pursuit battles, far more effective than linear combat because the British had a marked superiority of force, and the confidence to exploit it.

Once again naval attrition had triumphed, with the deeper resources of the British eventually overwhelming their rivals. After the battles of 1747, France had no more seaworthy ships, seamen, or money. Her naval effort had completely failed. Although French privateers took about 3,000 British merchant ships, a significant proportion of the fleet, the British annihilated French merchant shipping, crippling her economy and cutting the customs revenues that funded the war. Famine struck France once again in 1747. As the Anglo-Dutch-Austrian alliance had lost the war in Europe, with Marshal de Saxe overrunning Belgium and part of Holland, maritime victory provided a vital counterweight. After a hesitant start, seapower had become a critical factor in European politics. Consequently, the 1748 Treaty of Aix-la-Chapelle exchanged the Austrian Netherlands for Louisbourg. The French also returned Madras. They were pleased to get out of the war, recognizing that while their finances had failed, Britain could easily carry the burden of a maritime conflict. This peace, however, was only a breathing space.

NAVAL RECONSTRUCTION

For a variety of reasons, primarily those of domestic politics, Britain failed to keep pace with the build-up of the Bourbon fleets, but remained more than a match for either, and retained the doctrinal advantage of having a true battle fleet. However, her imperial position would depend on early and significant success at sea.

After the war the Royal Navy was overhauled to meet the new strategic situation. Global operations against evasive enemies who relied on fast squadrons of large two-decked battleships and frigates could not be countered by old-fashioned fleets of slow cruisers and small battleships designed for short-range operations in the Channel. New 74-gun two-deckers were built, carrying their guns high out of the water and sailing well, with stowage for long-range operations. As the best compromise between the various qualities demanded of a battleship and the available resources, the 74 would be the backbone of all major fleets between 1756 and 1805. The British also built new 90- and 100-gun three-deckers; France and Spain did not, abandoning any possibility of contesting command of the sea. It was a decision they would both regret and reverse. Similarly, French frigates were generally lighter and faster for their size than their British equivalents because, like their battleships, they required speed for evasion. Superior fair weather sailing was purchased at the cost of heavy weather sailing qualities and hull strength. Because the Royal Navy expected to conduct prolonged blockade and cruising operations, it built stronger ships.

For the French Navy, recovery from the disasters of 1746–7 was hampered by a rapid succession of ministers of the marine. This added a new layer of confusion to an already muddled situation. Throughout the reign of Louis XV, the navy lacked royal or national leadership, and had no clear role in a political environment dominated by European concerns. The service was heavily committed to colonial activities, which were of marginal importance at Versailles, and was crippled by an ageing officer corps, mounting debts and limited manpower. Between 1748 and 1756 the navy spent most of its budget on new construction, sending few ships to sea. This exacerbated a chronic weakness of the French fleet – limited sea experience. While much has been made of the superior technical education provided in France, few officers had the knowledge or application to profit from it, and it was no substitute for active service. Furthermore, it did not include any understanding of basic hygiene. In the three major wars of the mid century, the French Navy was ravaged by disease; typhus in 1746 and 1757–8, and bacillary dysentery in 1779–80.

In the mid 1750s the French, hitherto reliant on Swedish and English suppliers for iron guns, began to make a significant proportion of their own guns, but these never matched British guns in quality or quantity. The French guns were cast in small, primitive foundries, using metal from three separate furnaces to make a single 36-pounder gun. Such guns had a tendency to explode along fault lines between the different batches of metal. The problem was particularly acute when guns were fired rapidly over long periods, which led to a steady build-up of heat that weakened the metal. Guns cast from a single source would split, and those cast from mixed batches tended to burst, with serious consequences on crowded gun decks, where the low ceiling and nearby loose gunpowder could cause secondary explosions. British gunners fired faster because they were better trained and more experienced, but also because they had confidence in their guns. At close quarters the British would double-load their guns, firing two shots: French gunners dared not reply, and often abandoned their guns rather than risk being killed by them.

THE SEVEN YEARS WAR 1756–63

The Seven Years War arose out of the failure of Britain and France to settle the colonial boundaries of North America after 1748. Although Canada was of marginal interest to France, it was none the less a national asset. By contrast, the more populous British American colonies had real economic significance. Their trade was more valuable than that of the British sugar islands, with which they combined to make a strong economic unit. The land-hungry, expansionist and ambitious colonists continued to clash with the French, and their conflicts escalated into war. In January 1755 the British mobilized the navy, sent troops to counter the French build-up in Canada and ordered Admiral Boscawen to intercept a French troop convoy heading for Canada. Although Boscawen took three ships, missing the remainder in the fog on the Grand Banks, France did not declare war. Her fleet was too small to risk a conflict. Later in the year the British stepped up the pressure, seizing French merchant shipping. This was a masterstroke, imprisoning the cream of France's deep-sea mariners before they went on board a warship. The process of attrition, the key to success in war at sea, had been greatly accelerated. Even so, the French merely demanded compensation. Britain refused and finally declared war in May 1756. By 1758 the British held 20,000 French sailors. As France had only 50,000 registered seafarers at the start of the war, her choices at sea were greatly circumscribed. When another 10,000 men either died of typhus or had to be discharged as unfit for further service in 1757–8, the problem became overwhelming. In addition, the few remaining sailors refused to serve unless compelled, because the state simply could not pay them. Money, far more than fear of death or disease, determined the behaviour of French sailors.

Despite having the initiative, Britain began the war badly. Fear of invasion, and concern for politically sensitive trade, prompted Anson to keep too many ships in home waters. This left Admiral Sir John Byng (the son of Sir George), with a weak Mediterranean fleet. The French invaded Minorca in April, hoping to encourage Spain to join the conflict, and divert the British from other theatres. When they met off Minorca on 20 May, Byng attacked the equally matched French fleet of Admiral de la Galissonière, but despite his aggressive tactics he could not force a close

In the mid eighteenth century single-ship actions enabled officers to demonstrate both their skill and their honour. In this typical example on 6 October 1779 the frigates HMS Quebec *and the French* Surveillante *met off Brest. Both captains were bent on conquest and fought until their ships were disabled wrecks.* Quebec *then caught fire and blew up, killing almost all on board, including her captain, Farmer. Nelson had served under Farmer, and he was much admired throughout the service. (Richard Paton)*

action and the battle proved indecisive. Unfortunately Byng lacked strategic vision: he could not see that the French invasion, entirely dependent on the fleet, would be crippled by his mere presence. Instead, he held a council of war and retired to Gibraltar for repairs. The ministers needed a scapegoat for the loss of the island, and although the responsibility went higher, Byng was condemned by court martial and shot on the quarterdeck of his flagship. For all Voltaire's cynical observation that this was done '*pour encourager les autres*', the French service would have profited from the example. It had few flag officers of ability and the best, la Galissonière, died soon after the fall of Minorca.

The failure of British plans reflected a period of political turmoil. This began to change in July 1757 when a strong ministry was established by the Duke of Newcastle and the dynamic, aggressive William Pitt the Elder, who represented commercial interests. Newcastle provided consistent political support for a strategy developed by Anson and pushed through by Pitt. Reflecting the experience of the previous war, Anson destroyed the cohesion of the French position by blockading her fleets, isolating and capturing her colonial territories both to keep them and to use them as bargaining counters at the inevitable peace, and limiting any equivalent acquisitions by France in Europe. America was the priority, but Hanover and Europe had to be considered. Although the strategy combined imperial and continental elements, the ambitions were wholly imperial. Pitt used an army in Germany to protect the king's Hanoverian electorate, and launched amphibious raids on the French coast to draw resources away from the Rhine frontier. The German element of his programme, however, depended on Frederick II of Prussia. The Prussians were helped with a subsidy and a Hanoverian army, but Pitt refused to be drawn into war with Russia and Austria. There were no British interests at stake in central Europe.

Operations against Canada were delayed in 1757 by the appearance of a French fleet at Louisbourg. At this stage the Western Squadron had yet to take control of the sea approaches to Brest and the French

Atlantic ports. However, the return the French fleet to Brest in late 1757 proved to be a disaster on the scale of 1746, for it brought with it an epidemic of typhus that killed thousands and disabled the base and the fleet for months. In 1758 the Western Squadron took control of the French Atlantic coast, while Anson drilled the fleet up to his own high standards. In August Captain Howe led an amphibious expedition that destroyed the shipping and harbour at Cherbourg. Amphibious operations on the French coast were abandoned after the failure of an attack on St Malo. Harassing the French coast hardly seemed worthwhile when their armies had been driven out of Hanover and their colonies captured.

By launching a three-pronged invasion of Canada, via the St Lawrence seaway, the Hudson River and Lake Ontario, the British exploited their advantage of superior sea-based logistics and larger forces. Once Boscawen and Wolfe had taken Louisbourg in July 1758, along with six battleships, the main route into Canada was open. In 1759 Anson's protégé Admiral Saunders conveyed Wolfe's army to Quebec, his fleet led by John Jervis, later Earl St Vincent, with James Cook as one of the pilots. The conquest of Canada was the product of a truly global strategy.

By 1758 the inevitable loss of Canada prompted the French to revive plans to invade Britain, hoping to recover their colonies by a 'knock-out blow'. Although they could not compete at sea, the French hoped to combine their fleets on the Atlantic coast and escort 30,000 troops to land in the west of Scotland, then take the fleet round the north of Scotland to convoy a force from Normandy and Flanders to Essex, for a direct strike at London. This was exactly what Anson desired: it would provide an opportunity to destroy the French fleet.

Anson's commanders did not disappoint. In the Mediterranean, Boscawen, with fifteen battleships, intercepted la Clue's fleet of seven as they passed the Straits of Gibraltar on 18 August 1759, five others having broken off to Cádiz. One ship was captured, two escaped into the Atlantic and four ran aground off the Portuguese city of Lagos, where they were taken or burnt the following day, despite Portuguese neutrality. In July a mortar flotilla commanded by Captain Sir George Rodney bombarded the invasion shipping at Le Havre to delay the French operation. Hawke and Anson had developed a system to supply the fleet at sea with live cattle, fresh vegetables and beer, allowing the fleet to stay at sea for six months – a massive increase in seapower's sustainability. Hawke exploited this system to blockade the French in Brest and cut them off from supplies of naval stores, which were being delivered by neutral, largely Dutch, ships. New, more rigorous, definitions of contraband were developed to support this strategy.

Admiral Conflans put to sea on 14 November with twenty-one battleships after a strong westerly gale (which he believed had blown Hawke back to Plymouth) had enabled a French squadron from the West Indies to get into harbour, and provided him with additional seamen. He hoped to pick up the troop transports in the Loire estuary and sail to Scotland without a battle. However, he was soon located by Hawke's cruisers. Hawke left Torbay with twenty-three battleships as soon as the gale abated. He was well aware of the French plans.

Early on 20 November the fleets were in visual contact, and Conflans tried to escape into the treacherous coastal waters of Quiberon Bay. Here the superior seamanship and confidence of the Royal Navy proved decisive. In a full gale, and with the light fading fast, Hawke's fleet, led by Howe in the 74-gun *Magnanime*, closed up with the French, relying on them to avoid the navigational hazards. The French rearguard was quickly overpowered: one ship foundered when she opened her lower deck gunports, another was sunk by a single broadside from Hawke's first rate 100-gun flagship, *Royal George*, and two more surrendered. The French formation broke up: eight ships escaped to Rochefort, and seven more ran into the shallow River Vilaine, abandoning their guns. When night fell the fleets anchored. In the morning Conflans's *Le Soleil Royal* found herself among the British fleet, so she cut her cables, went aground and was burnt like her namesake in 1692. Although the British *Essex* and *Resolution* were wrecked, and Hawke was dissatisfied with the result, this was that rarest of events at sea, a decisive battle, for Quiberon destroyed the last vestiges of the French Navy's financial credit. Arsenal workers were not paid, so ships were not built or repaired. By October 1759 the government was bankrupt and naval operations ceased for lack of money. If France could not develop the financial strength to build, maintain and operate a large fleet for a long war she could not hope to defeat Britain. No more French fleets went to sea before the end of the war.

As in 1747, the Western Squadron had secured command of the sea by wearing down the French fleet. There was little the French could have done, even if they had had ships to fit out and man. This remarkable performance, the culmination of a sustained six-month blockade of Brest, was based on the effective defeat of scurvy by the regular supply of fresh victuals, and the rotation of ships to Plymouth and Torbay for rest, repair and recuperation.

Having secured their war aims, the British captured the French West Indian islands to 'beat the French into a peace', as Pitt put it. In the absence of any significant opposition at sea, these attacks could be launched quickly, in the 'healthy' season, relying on overwhelming force to secure an easy victory. Guadeloupe fell in 1759, Dominica in 1761 and Martinique in 1762. The French West Indian economy was further disrupted by the seizure of the slave stations at Senegal and Goree. In June 1761 a combined operation took the island of Belle-Île as a bargaining counter for the peace negotiations.

In India the politico-military success of Robert Clive in securing control of the immense revenues of Bengal was based on seapower. Calcutta and the French enclave at Chandernagore were taken by the fleet in January 1757. French attempts to reverse these successes were blocked by a succession of indecisive, destructive battles in which Commodore George Pocock forced the French Admiral d'Ache to leave the coast in search of supplies, while the British, with a local base at Madras and a dockyard at Bombay, were able to remain on station. Command of the sea again gave the British a decisive advantage.

The battle of Quiberon Bay, 20 November 1759

The fruits of a global strategy. The British conquest of Canada in 1759 forced the French to change their strategy. Unable to assemble a force capable of recovering the province they elected to try an ambitious counterstroke in Europe. If they could combine their Brest and Toulon fleets, and escort an army to Britain, they might recover Canada in London, much as Pitt had boasted of conquering it in Germany. Instead the movement led to the destruction of both fleets at Lagos and then at Quiberon Bay.

1. Conflans retreats into Quiberon Bay, despite the danger of reefs and banks. Hawke follows and begins to overhaul the French fleet

2. The British fleet, 38 ships, engages the French, 26 ships. Despite heavy weather and the chance of being caught on a lee shore Hawke destroys seven French ships and scatters their fleet. He loses two ships after the battle

3. Seven French ships escape into the River Vilaine's estuary where they run aground

4. A group of surviving French ships run south and enter the River Charente where they are then blockaded by units of the British fleet

Quiberon

Battle of Quiberon Bay
20 November 1759

Q u i b e r o n   B a y

The death of King Ferdinand in 1759 brought his half-brother Charles III to the throne of Spain. Charles loathed the British, having been humiliated by them in 1742 while king of Naples. Although the opportunity for a combined Bourbon effort had passed, the signature of a new Bourbon 'Family Compact' in August 1761 was a clear threat, and Pitt argued for another pre-emptive strike. Anson provided a grand plan to take the port of Havana, the greatest fortress in the New World. In October the Cabinet, arguing that such an act would only serve to increase international hatred of Britain's dominion of the oceans and believing that the culminating point of victory had been reached, rejected Pitt's advice. Pitt resigned. However, Spain declared war in early 1762,

The capture of Belle-Île in 1761 by a combined force under Commodore Augustus Keppel and Colonel Hodgson was part of Pitt's strategy to force the French to make peace. He intended to use the island to secure the return of Minorca. The operation was relatively simple for the by now experienced British forces; sea control, an effective landing and a superior army were enough. The fortress surrendered on 8 June, after a breach was made in the wall. (Dominic Serres)

but, despite building 80,000 tons of new battleships since 1748, her fleet did not dare to confront the Royal Navy at sea. After Lagos and Quiberon there could be no doubt that the British had the right doctrine, the right officers and men, and the right ships. Anson's plan to capture Havana was adopted after all, although he did not live to see it carried into effect.

Transport fleets from Britain, the Windward Islands and North America met off the western tip of St Domingo. The combined force then secured strategic surprise by using the Old Bahama Channel along the north coast of Cuba, rather than coming around the western tip of the island as the Spanish had anticipated. General the Earl of Albemarle commanded 11,000 troops in 200 transports, escorted by twenty battleships and ten other warships under Admiral Sir George Pocock and Albemarle's brother Admiral Keppel. As the defences of Havana were considered too strong for a naval assault, the troops landed, with naval gunfire support, on 7 June 1762. The army seized the high ground commanding the city and the key fortress of El Morro. Once they had recovered from their surprise, the Spanish put up a stout resistance, relying on the 'sickly season', which began in August, for their salvation. The siege of El Morro was assisted by naval bombardments and a naval brigade. It finally fell on 30 July, a fitting testimony to the ability of well-built forts to delay superior forces. The British then attacked the city, aided by 4,000 fresh American troops. After a brief bombardment on 12 August the Spanish capitulated. Although the siege had been properly conducted, the over-long operation exposed the men to disease, and nearly 5,000 troops died, together with 800 sailors, most of whom had served ashore in the batteries. A Spanish fleet of twelve battleships was either captured or sunk, and the city ransomed. The prize money totalled £737,000, Albemarle's share of which rebuilt his family's fortune.

Despite the human cost, Havana was a masterpiece of amphibious warfare in the age of sail, and built on the experience of earlier, less fortunate, campaigns. On the opposite side of the world, a combined operation between the Royal Navy and the East India Company captured and ransomed another outpost of the Spanish empire, Manila.

Perhaps the most remarkable achievement of the British war effort had been manning the fleet. An estimated 184,893 seamen and marines served in the Royal Navy during the Seven Years War; 1,512 men were killed in action or died of their wounds, about 40,000 deserted, 34,000 were demobilized, and almost 60,000 died of disease or were discharged as unfit for service. To replace this steady drain of human resources required a conscious effort, ruthless determination and a very strong maritime labour market. France and Spain combined could not equal this performance. They could not find 184,000 sailors, even

Combined operations. *The boats of the fleet, filled with troops, alongside HMS* Alcide, *prepare to follow up the explosion of a mine under the land defences of El Morro Castle, Havana, 30 July 1762. El Morro, the most powerful fort in the New World, was the key to the defence of the city. It was stormed by the army that day.*

allowing for a large degree of skill dilution in the crews of large ships, and lacked the finances to retain as many men as the British.

The Peace of Paris in 1763 reflected the fact that Britain, with her chain of imperial, colonial and commercial bases, had become a true world power. Britain took Canada, Florida and Senegal, handing back Havana, Manila, the French sugar islands and Belle-Île. Spain evacuated Portugal. France and Spain had paid a high price for defeat, high enough to make revenge a powerful factor in the post-war policy, but not so high as to make their recovery impossible. More significantly, by removing the Bourbon threat from the North American colonies, Britain's relationship with the colonists was transformed. Where the events of 1755 and 1756 had led many colonists to fear an invasion by the French and their Indian allies, the peace led many to question the need to pay for any security forces, and they resented the British commercial legislation that raised the necessary funds for their protection. Seapower and effective coalitions had given Britain mastery of the colonial world, and a powerful voice in Europe. Her power was now so ubiquitous as to annoy the whole of Europe, together with many of her own colonists.

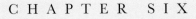

CHAPTER SIX

Reverse and Recovery: Britain versus the World 1776–82

The battle of the Saintes, 12 April 1782. A detail from a painting of the Saintes, showing Hood's Barfleur engaging de Grasse's Ville de Paris. Although his flagship was crippled the French admiral would only surrender to another flag officer, and by the time Hood arrived the French crew had suffered terrible casualties. (Thomas Luny)

Reverse and Recovery: Britain Versus the World 1776–82

LONG BEFORE THE END of the Seven Years War British success had persuaded France and Spain to shift their strategic focus away from Europe. The third Bourbon 'Family Compact' of August 1761 was an imperial alliance, without the European dimension of the two previous treaties. After the disasters of 1762 France only kept Spain in the alliance by transferring the western half of Louisiana to her, as compensation for the loss of Florida. Furthermore, the two powers took diametrically opposed views of the alliance. Spain saw it as a defensive system to protect her sprawling, vulnerable empire, but France, led by Louis XV's principal minister Choiseul, wanted to reduce British power and recover her prestige, a task that would require the combined naval strength of the two powers.

With their economies in ruins, the Bourbon powers were in no position to support a war in 1763, but both countries began a steady accumulation of naval strength. French dockyards were modernized for the first time since Colbert, a school of naval medicine was rather belatedly opened in 1768, and warship designs were standardized. French cities, guilds and merchants funded new battleships, which were accordingly named *Ville de Paris* and *Etats de Bourgogne*. The Spanish effort was less spectacular but, like that of France, it would be sustained down to the outbreak of the French Revolutionary war in 1793. By this time both nations had doubled the size of their battle fleets from the low point of 1763, but until 1778 the Bourbons persisted in their doctrine of avoiding battle. They built only three three-decked ships before the American war, a choice they were to reverse in the following decade. The real weaknesses of the Bourbon revival were the lack of money and sea experience. Financial pressure explains why the French did not send a training squadron to sea until 1774, while the Spanish rarely fitted out more than a handful of ships, and never for mere exercise. This omission weakened the Bourbon naval effort, giving the British a critical advantage.

The main British dockyards at Portsmouth and Plymouth were modernized, stocks of naval stores, from timber to iron, were increased, and new technologies were adopted. Two would have a significant impact on the next war. Copper-sheathing the hull of ships poisoned marine-boring molluscs like the tropical *teredo navalis* that ruined timber, and other marine growths that slowed the ship. The other breakthrough came in artillery technology, with the introduction of the 'carronade'. The Royal Navy used 32-pounder carronades to replace 6-pounder long guns on the upper decks of warships, this increase in close-range firepower complementing British tactical doctrine. These technical advantages would be critical because the Royal Navy was no longer numerically superior to the combined Bourbon fleets.

Despite the gradual Bourbon build-up, Britain maintained her commanding position in the global economy, using her fleet as the strong arm of her diplomacy. In 1770, when the Spanish governor of Buenos Aires expelled British troops from the Falkland Islands, the British mobilized and demanded restitution. Louis XV dismissed Choiseul and persuaded Spain to back down. The sudden interest in the Falklands reflected the view that they were the key to the Pacific, and Spanish weakness in that ocean had been demonstrated by the collapse of Manila in 1762. For all the high-minded 'scientific' motives ascribed to Pacific exploration in this period, the real objects remained empire, trade and power. The three great voyages of Captain James Cook (1728–79) between 1768 and 1779 opened the Pacific for trade and unveiled a new continent for settlement. They also demonstrated that improved attention to the health of the seamen would avoid the ravages of scurvy. French and Spanish voyages also made important contributions, but not on the scale of those led by Cook.

After 1760 British armed forces in the Americas, for so long a source of security against the French and the Native Americans, became objectionable to a people who had no desire to pay for them. The Royal

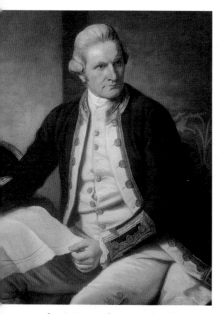

The greatest navigator of the age, James Cook opened the Pacific for trade, settlement and empire. He also established a tradition of excellence in navigation, survey and hydrography that has endured to this day. (Nathaniel Dance)

Navy imposed the unpopular import duties that sparked the 'Boston Tea Party' in 1773, and by 1775 the American colonies were in open rebellion, setting the British an immense strategic and logistical challenge. Troops had to be transported and supplied 3,000 miles from their main base, in stark contrast to previous wars in the Americas, where local support, logistics and troops had been critical. Furthermore, the instruments of British power were of questionable utility in the new circumstances. An army prepared for war in Europe, against regular opposition, abiding by the laws and customs of war, found it hard to engage an enemy who was prepared to sacrifice territory for time, and had no true centre of gravity outside Washington's army. The Royal Navy provided logistics support and strategic mobility for the army, attempted to impose an effective blockade to stop the import of arms and gunpowder, and tried to deal with American privateers and state warships. These conflicting demands, and the limited naval force available, lacking both men and ships, restricted its impact.

Despite these difficulties the British came close to success in 1776 and 1777, gravely weakening the American effort. The capture of New York in 1776, which halted French plans to recognize the colonists, was a masterpiece of amphibious power projection. The troops went ashore in purpose-built landing craft under naval gunfire support, while the co-operation of Admiral Lord Howe and his younger brother General Sir William Howe was a major element in the victory. However, the Howe brothers believed the war could be ended by American submission, and did not exploit their opportunity to destroy Washington's army.

In 1777 the British armies in Quebec and New York needed to be co-ordinated to achieve maximum effect. Yet, while Howe in New York planned to take Philadelphia by sea, General John Burgoyne was expecting him to advance up the Hudson River to meet his thrust from Canada. Burgoyne, having secured command of Lake Champlain, was cut off and defeated at Saratoga when he advanced inland. Saratoga was critical: it destroyed the prestige of the British Army, hitherto unbeaten, and persuaded the French to intervene. The seaborne attack on Philadelphia took Howe's army off the field for two months and tied up the entire fleet, ending any attempt to impose a blockade.

From 1774 French policy had been handled for the new king, Louis XVI, by the Comte de Vergennes. Vergennes shared Choiseul's desire to humble Britain, as the prelude to a new Franco-British alignment on a basis of equality. He thought the loss of the American colonies, especially their maritime resources and seafaring population, would achieve his aims. From 1776 the French actively supported the rebels by shipping arms and allowing privateers to use French harbours, while mobilizing their navy. Despite this, British ministers tried to maintain good relations with France, content to match French mobilization without trying to deter it. Full-scale mobilization linked to a clear statement of British demands was their best hope of preserving peace. The only benefit of this weak policy was to delay the intervention of Spain by a year. In the interval, Vergennes cultivated the minor maritime powers, especially the Dutch and the Danes, by supporting the doctrine of 'free ships, free goods'. He wanted to increase pressure on Britain, and secure access to naval stores once war broke out.

The successful French naval mobilization enabled Vergennes to react decisively to news of Saratoga, which reached Europe in October 1777.

While Saratoga demonstrated that the rebellion would continue, it also made Vergennes fear the British would compromise with the Americans. The only reason for French delay was the uncertain response of Spain. The Spanish, unhappy with their subordinate role in the Compact, were unenthusiastic. They recognized that supporting the rebels would send a dangerous signal to the Spanish-American colonies. Consequently, Spain never recognized the rebels and provided no direct support. Even her co-operation with France was inconsistent. Vergennes only secured an offensive alliance in April 1779, in return for French support to recover Gibraltar, Minorca and Florida. These limited, territorial objectives were wholly out of step with the political aims of the French.

The intervention of France in July 1778 complicated British decision-making. It also paralysed efforts to blockade the American coast, forcing Lord Howe to concentrate his fleet and respond to movements of the more powerful French fleet which suddenly appeared off New York. Although Howe had the skill to protect the army ashore, he could not bring the French to battle. Angered by ministerial criticism of his brother, Howe resigned, depriving the service of its leading tactician for much of the war. This left the North American command to a succession of mediocre admirals, who compounded their weaknesses by quarrelling with the generals. After 1778, naval operations in American waters were subordinated to the Anglo-French war in the West Indies. For most of the year the main fleets operated around the Sugar Islands, only coming north during the summer hurricane season.

In European waters the British sent a powerful fleet of thirty battleships under Admiral Sir Augustus Keppel, the last of Anson's protégés, to secure command of the Western Approaches. However, Keppel's fleet had been mobilized at the last moment, missing the chance to deter France, and to prepare for war. The French fleet under Admiral d'Orvilliers, although slightly smaller (with twenty-seven battleships), had been at sea longer. After four days of manoeuvring, in which Keppel tried to bring the French to battle, and d'Orvilliers waited for a tactical advantage that would allow him to oblige, the fleets finally engaged on 27 July off Cape Ushant. The stakes were high. A British victory would re-establish the strategic grip of Anson's Western Squadron, cutting American supplies and French operations in the West Indies. A British defeat would open the country to invasion, leave her colonies at the mercy of the French, and bring Spain into the war.

At dawn on 27 July 1778 the French were to windward in a regular line; the British were converging with them as far as the wind allowed, in an ill-formed bow and quarter line, Admiral Sir Hugh Palliser making no effort to close a gap of nearly 3 miles between his squadron and Keppel's flagship, HMS *Victory*. The cautious French admiral interpreted this as an attempt to get to windward of his rear, and reversed course. This put both fleets in some disorder. Keppel would

The most famous warship of the age, HMS Victory. *During the American War, she served as flagship in home waters. She is seen here in 1793, carrying the flag of Admiral Lord Hood. A decade later Nelson, who admired Hood above all other admirals, would take her to immortality. (Monamy Swaine)*

not risk the loss of time required to organize his fleet into line, being anxious that the French should not escape. After a squall temporarily separated the fleets, Keppel tacked his fleet to engage on an opposite course; the British were still overly extended in an irregular line, and the French were more compact. The action began at 11 a.m. with the fleets passing at a combined speed of 6–8 knots. From the windward side, the French deliberately fired into the British rigging, crippling several ships. The British fired into the French ships, inflicting 700 casualties to the 500 they suffered. Thick smoke quickly obscured the battlefield. D'Orvilliers had a better view ahead than Keppel, and his van weathered Keppel's rear; he ordered it to tack and continue the engagement. This was much too daring for the divisional commander, who put back to consult the admiral and missed the opportunity. In marked contrast, the commander of the British van squadron rounded the French rear on his own initiative. Keppel approved, but did not follow, wearing round to support four damaged ships that had fallen out of line and that were, he thought, in danger from the French. Thereafter Keppel, with his fleet in a confused huddle, tried to form a line and attack. Palliser, however, whether from incompetence or from malice, failed to get into station despite repeated orders. The French did not try to resume the fight, as they had had quite enough of close-quarters action with the 'terrible fire of the British three-deckers'. While d'Orvilliers had two three-decked ships in the battle, Keppel had seven. The clumsy 90-gun ships that so alarmed the French also denied Keppel the speed to chase his enemy; any fleet that relied on them would catch only an incompetent enemy.

Ushant demonstrated better than any other battle that the line was the basis of all tactics. Without a well-ordered line, Keppel could not exploit his superior firepower to break the French formation and secure victory in a close-quarters mêlée, where his 90-gun ships would easily overpower the French two-deckers. While Keppel had forced a battle, he had not been able to force a conclusion, a result which suited the French.

Ushant was the first Anglo-French sea battle in European waters to be fought along regular lines since Toulon in 1744. It repeated the lesson of Toulon, that fleets going into battle in disorder are at a great disadvantage. Keppel had the offensive spirit of his mentor Anson, but lacked the disciplined fleet needed to exploit his opportunities and the signalling capacity to make his views understood. Although Ushant was a wasted opportunity, it revitalized tactical thinking and prompted the development of a new signalling system. After the battle political divisions within the Royal Navy led to courts martial for the Whig Keppel and the Tory Palliser; both were acquitted, but Keppel refused to serve again, and Palliser was sent ashore.

In June 1779 Spain joined the war, and immediately attacked Minorca and Gibraltar. A combined Channel fleet of sixty-six ships, with another twenty Spanish battleships in reserve, was assembled to attack Portsmouth. However, the combined fleet proved unwieldy and ineffective. The Spanish ships, well built but weakly armed and badly manned, lacked the tactical skill to work with the French. Even before the fleets met, the health of the French crews began to break down. Recognizing the threat, the British fleet gradually increased from thirty to forty battleships under the elderly Admiral Sir Charles Hardy, advised by his brilliant flag captain, Richard Kempenfelt. They would mirror Tourville's campaign of 1690 (see chapter three) with Hardy, like Herbert before him, conducting a competent delaying campaign, observing the allies but refusing battle. After long delays getting the Spanish ships to sea, the combined fleet entered the Channel late, with a growing sick list, and left early in the grip of a dysentery epidemic that killed thousands. Unable to meet, let alone fight, the British, their objective shifted from Portsmouth to Plymouth and then Falmouth, but they could not attack in the presence of an unbeaten enemy. The allies did not have the ability to force a battle, or the confidence that they could defeat a British fleet with so many three-deckers. Having wasted half the season assembling an overwhelming numerical superiority, the Bourbons could neither sustain their effort nor supply the fleet with fresh provisions.

On 23 September 1779, off Flamborough Head on the east coast of Britain, a squadron of Franco-American privateers led by Captain John Paul Jones in the *Bonhomme Richard* encountered the British Baltic trade convoy, escorted by Captain Richard Pearson in HMS *Serapis*, a 44-gun ship, with one smaller ship. Pearson properly placed his warships between the convoy and the enemy, enabling the convoy to escape. He then brought Jones to action, and rapidly overpowered his makeshift ex-Indiaman flagship. Pearson, however, lacked imagination. He allowed Jones's sinking ship to close with him; the Americans then boarded and captured the *Serapis* just before their own vessel sank. Although the battle made Jones a national hero, and the 'father' of the United States Navy, the escape of the convoy secured Pearson a rich reward and a knighthood: there could be no stronger evidence for the economic backbone of the Royal Navy. American privateers proved to be a constant problem for the British, particularly at the focal points of the Atlantic trade.

That winter Admiral Sir George Rodney, commanding twenty-two battleships, escorted a relief convoy to Gibraltar. On the night of 16 January 1780 he encountered eleven Spanish battleships under Admiral Langara off Cape St Vincent, and captured six of them in a chase action. Having re-supplied Gibraltar, Rodney took his fleet to the West Indies, where the French had captured Grenada and St Vincent. On 17 April 1780 Rodney, with twenty ships, brought Admiral de Guichen, with twenty-four, to battle off Martinique. Rodney wanted to concentrate on the rear of the French fleet, while holding off the van and centre. Unfortunately his subordinates did not understand his concept, and the battle degenerated into a simple linear firefight, which de Guichen broke off when Rodney's disabled flagship drifted through the French line. The failure of Rodney's plan revealed the poverty of British doctrine and the weakness of their signalling systems.

In 1781 the French Admiral de Grasse exploited his superiority to capture St Lucia and Tobago before moving north to isolate Lord Cornwallis's army at Yorktown. Rodney returned to England to recover

The 'Moonlight battle', 16 January 1780. On his way to relieve Gibraltar Rodney
encountered the Spanish off Cape St Vincent, and immediately launched a pursuit,
despite the rising wind and darkness, cutting the Spanish off from their base.
Attacked in succession the Spanish lost six ships taken, while another blew up.
(Thomas Luny)

his health, leaving his fleet, under the uninspired Admiral Graves, to engage the French off the Virginia Capes on 5 September 1781. The battle was tactically indecisive, Graves lacking the insight and skill to seize the fleeting opportunity given by de Grasse. After Cornwallis's capitulation at Yorktown Britain effectively abandoned the war for America. Henceforth all efforts were devoted to the West Indies and Gibraltar.

When Rodney returned to the West Indies, both fleets had around thirty ships, although Rodney had more three-deckers. De Grasse was planning to invade Jamaica and needed to escort a large Bourbon troop convoy. Off Dominica on 9 April he exploited a calm to cut off Hood's division, but failed to destroy it before Rodney came up.

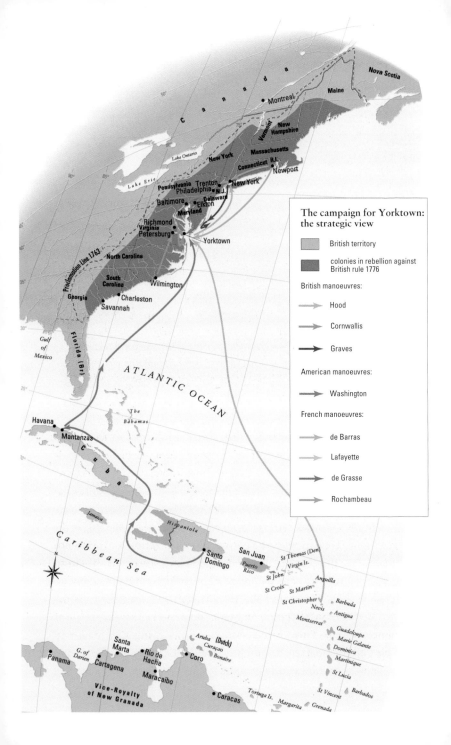

The campaign for Yorktown:
the strategic view

British territory

colonies in rebellion against
British rule 1776

British manoeuvres:

Hood

Cornwallis

Graves

American manoeuvres:

Washington

French manoeuvres:

de Barras

Lafayette

de Grasse

Rochambeau

Canada

Nova Scotia

Montreal
Maine
Vermont
New Hampshire
Lake Ontario
New York
Massachusetts
Connecticut R.I.
Lake Erie
Newport
Pennsylvania Trenton
Philadelphia New York
N.J.
Baltimore Delaware
Elkton
Maryland
Richmond
Virginia
Petersburg
Yorktown
Proclamation Line 1763
North Carolina
South Carolina
Wilmington
Georgia
Charleston
Savannah

Gulf
of
Mexico

Florida (Br)

ATLANTIC OCEAN

The
Bahamas

Havana
Mantanzas
Cuba

Jamaica
Hispaniola

Caribbean Sea

Santo
Domingo

San Juan
Puerto
Rico
St Thomas (Den)
Virgin Is.
St John
St Croix
St Martin
Anguilla
St Christopher
Nevis
Barbuda
Montserrat
Antigua
Guadeloupe
Marie Galante
Dominica
Martinica
St Lucia
St Vincent
Barbados
Tortuga Is. Margarita Grenada

N

Panama
G. of
Darien
Santa
Marta
Rio de
Hacha
Cartagena
Maracaibo
Coro
Aruba (Dutch)
Curaçao
Bonaire

Vice-Royalty
of New Granada
Caracas

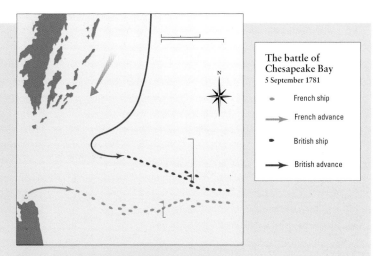

The battle of
Chesapeake Bay
5 September 1781

- French ship

→ French advance

• British ship

→ British advance

STRATEGIC VICTORY

Every autumn the main fleets went north to avoid the West Indian hurricanes.
In 1781 the French arrived first, secured control of Chesapeake Bay, and on
5 September 1781 beat off the British under the uninspired Graves. Graves's
failure led to the surrender of Lord Cornwallis's army at Yorktown.

On 12 April 1782, the fleets, now thirty-six British to thirty-two French, met again in the Saintes passage. Poor seamanship in de Grasse's fleet brought on a battle. This time Rodney was able to bring his whole force to bear. The fleets began to pass on opposite courses at 7 a.m., the British heading north, the French south. The British were sailing in close formation, in a compact line less than two thirds the length of the French, who were straggling into action and were not properly formed up. After two hours the French formation began to fragment under close-range fire when a sudden shift in the wind enabled Rodney, Hood and the van division to break through the French line at separate points in quick succession. This 'breaking of the line' destroyed the French formation, allowing the British to impose close-quarters action, where their three-deckers and carronades were devastatingly effective. As Rodney's *Formidable* broke through, officers on her quarterdeck could see French gun crews running into the hold. The fleet physician Sir Gilbert Blane observed, 'the French fire slackens as we approach, and it is totally silent when we are close alongside'. The French gunners knew that they would be overpowered at close range, and feared their own guns as much as British fire. Within minutes *Formidable* had reduced the 74-gun *Glorieux* to a dismasted wreck, while the *Diadem* was hit hard and fell off the wind, causing the ships astern to lose formation. After four hours the French fleet began to break up and make off. By 6 p.m. de Grasse had been captured aboard his flagship, the *Ville de Paris*, along with four other French battleships. When British officers went aboard to take the surrender they were astonished to find the blood on

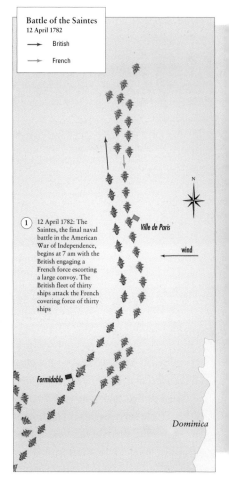

Battle of the Saintes
12 April 1782

→ British

→ French

(1) 12 April 1782: The Saintes, the final naval battle in the American War of Independence, begins at 7 am with the British engaging a French force escorting a large convoy. The British fleet of thirty ships attack the French covering force of thirty ships

N

Ville de Paris

wind

Formidable

Dominica

the upper deck ran into their shoes. *Ville de Paris* alone had 400 men killed, more than the entire British fleet. While Rodney had not planned to 'break the line', he had the skill to seize the chance. He then failed to exploit his success, enraging his second, the acerbic and brilliant Hood, who argued that a determined pursuit would have completed the victory. This was true – five crippled French ships got

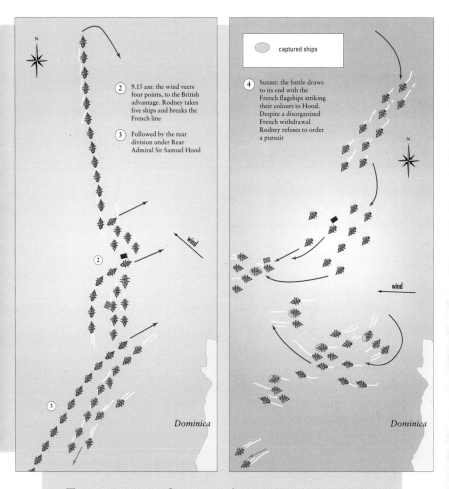

captured ships

2) 9.15 am: the wind veers four points, to the British advantage. Rodney takes five ships and breaks the French line

3) Followed by the rear division under Rear Admiral Sir Samuel Hood

4) Sunset: the battle draws to its end with the French flagships striking their colours to Hood. Despite a disorganized French withdrawal Rodney refuses to order a pursuit

wind

wind

Dominica

Dominica

THE BATTLE OF THE SAINTES, 12 APRIL 1782

Finally able to bring his full force to bear, Rodney exploited French mistakes to force a close-range battle, used a shift in the wind to destroy their formation, and exploited the close-quarters firepower of carronades to shatter de Grasse's fleet, capturing the French admiral. This great victory restored British confidence after a troublesome war.

Left: *The man who might have made the difference. Samuel, Lord Hood (1724–1816), the one officer of genius to serve in this war, was only second in command at Chesapeake, and made little effort to help his pedestrian commander. Once in command he demonstrated exactly how to fight such battles at St Kitts in January 1782, comprehensively out-thinking de Grasse.*

Below: *The Saintes, 12 April 1782. Rodney secured a great victory because his whole fleet was animated by the same aggressive spirit, a common doctrine based on close-range battle. Once the linear battle had broken his faster ships, carronades and, in some ships, flintlocks gave the British a real advantage. However, Hood was not satisfied, and his ideas would dominate the next war. (Thomas Luny)*

away. When Hood was finally released to chase he took two more battleships.

The missed opportunity of 1782 would influence the admirals of the next generation from William Cornwallis and James de Saumarez, who commanded ships that day, to Nelson, who learnt the lesson from his mentor, Hood, and his friend Cornwallis. While the Saintes was an incomplete triumph it saved Jamaica for the British, provided them with a much needed morale-boosting victory to take to the peace negotiations, restored their mastery at sea, restated the value of 'battle'-based doctrine, and introduced a new generation of officers to fleet action.

The situation in European waters had been complicated by the Dutch insistence on trading with the American colonists. Consequently, in December 1780, Britain declared war, and on 5 August 1781 a savage, bloody action took place on the Dogger Bank between the escorts of two convoys. The British were slightly more successful here and their convoy got through, while the Dutch lost a battleship and put back to port. More significantly, the war allowed the British to capture the Dutch West Indian island of St Eustasius, the key supply centre for the rebels, and, as a result, to annihilate Dutch shipping. Unable to defend their convoys, despite recent efforts to restore their fleet, the Dutch suffered heavily. In truth the stakes in sea warfare had risen so far that a battle fleet the same size as the one they deployed in 1652 was now only equal to 16 per cent of the British fleet. The lesson was clear: second-class navies would be crushed.

In the middle of 1781 a combined fleet of forty-nine battleships appeared in the Channel, but they achieved nothing. In December Kempenfelt, who had now been promoted to rear admiral, sailing in HMS *Victory* with twelve ships, took fifteen transports from a convoy escorted by a superior French fleet. De Guichen, caught ahead and to leeward of his convoy, could only watch while Kempenfelt secured his prizes. Kempenfelt's skill presented a stark contrast to the very ordinary performances of Hardy, Graves and others.

In February 1782 Bourbon forces finally captured Minorca, the only first-class natural harbour in the Mediterranean under British control, and built up for a decisive attack on Gibraltar, which had survived the blockade through the timely arrival of the two relief convoys. However, Howe agreed to take command of the Channel fleet in April, and the Western Squadron strategy began to function properly. French convoys heading for the East Indies were crippled, and British trade was protected. When the allies deployed a fleet of fifty battleships, Howe, with only half as many, conducted a skilled defence, which included sailing through the dangerous waters of the Scillies. By the middle of the year it was necessary to re-supply Gibraltar, and Howe, in the

Victory, assembled the fleet and transports at Spithead. Here on 27 August the *Royal George* sank, taking with her Kempenfelt and 900 men, women and children, for many families were on board. The loss was caused entirely by poor seamanship. She was being heeled over for a minor repair below the waterline when the officers on deck allowed her to get too far over. However, the sea officers persuaded the court martial that the ship's bottom had fallen out, thus passing the blame on to the dockyard.

Despite the disaster Howe conducted a masterly relief, getting the convoy into Gibraltar Bay, in the face of a larger allied force, without a battle. Howe considered this his greatest achievement, but it also reflected the demoralization of the allies. On 13 September they had launched their grand attack from the sea, using ten specially constructed Spanish floating batteries. These had very thick sides, with water pumps to keep them wet. However, the pumps clogged and red-hot shot fired from the fortress set nine batteries on fire; the last was destroyed by a British boat attack.

A national catastrophe. On 27 August 1782 HMS Royal George, *which had carried Hawke's flag at Quiberon, sank with heavy loss of life at Spithead, in full view of the fleet, and of the base at Portsmouth, as a direct result of an ill-advised attempt to effect a minor underwater repair. The real cause of her loss quickly became obscured in a smokescreen of legend. (Thomas Buttersworth)*

HMS Victory, bearing the flag of Lord Howe, arriving off Gibraltar, 16 September 1782, for the third and final relief of the besieged fortress. Howe always considered this feat, in the face of a superior Franco-Spanish force, to be the high point of his career.

In 1781 the French sent a fleet to the East Indies, hoping to recover their power in India. While on passage Admiral Suffren (1729–88), a bold, aggressive, battle-orientated officer, completely out of step with his service, crippled a British force intending to seize Cape Town from the Dutch. He then conducted a daring campaign on the coast of India. While Suffren had considerable tactical skill, and understood the importance of concentrating his attack against part of the British fleet, his efforts were negated by the solid qualities of the British Admiral Sir Edward Hughes and his fleet. While Suffren's ships were badly handled, and some of his captains were mutinous or cowardly, Hughes's fleet invariably formed a close-knit line, and out-fought the superior numbers that Suffren's tactical finesse threw against them. Suffren kept the French campaign alive by his ability and energy, patching up his ships miles from any base, but apart from the seizure of Trincomalee he was unable to defeat Hughes. The battles between these two resolute men form a fascinating page in the history of naval tactics, but they had no effect on the decisive defeat of French power in India. Suffren has been much celebrated, but this reflects more on the failure of his contemporaries than on his own success.

When peace negotiations opened in late 1782 the Anglo-French issues were easily solved. Both nations wanted peace: the French were bankrupt (as were the Spanish), while Britain had spent huge sums to no effect. Howe's relief of Gibraltar had broken Spanish resistance. Over the winter of 1782–3 Britain recognized the loss of the American colonies, while France acquired Tobago, Senegal and some fishery concessions off Newfoundland. Spain retained Minorca and Florida, but the Dutch gave up a trading station in Ceylon.

Vergennes's plan to weaken Britain by breaking the Atlantic basis of her maritime economic strength had failed. After the peace Anglo-American trade recovered rapidly, soon passing the pre-war level. French finances, however, did not recover, leading to political turmoil and ultimately to revolution. This was the true cost of intervention. Within a generation the revolutionary contagion had also destroyed the Spanish-American empire. Elsewhere, the loss of America influenced the pace of development in the Pacific. The search for naval stores and the need for new convict settlements led to the colonization of Australia by the First Fleet that landed at Botany Bay in 1788.

For many years it was argued that Britain lost America because she was unable to match the naval power of France and Spain when they were not distracted by European wars. In fact, Britain defeated the navies of France, Spain, Holland and the rebels. She lost America because the colonists were determined to assert their independence, and the British government could not break their will to resist. This process was complicated by Bourbon intervention, but once the British gave up trying to reconquer America, after Yorktown, they rapidly reasserted their pre-eminence at sea. France and Spain were simply too poor to fight a long war, while Britain, wealthier by far, could. Once the war resumed the pattern of the earlier Anglo-Bourbon struggles – limited wars for colonial territory, with the occasional half-hearted threat to invade Britain thrown in – money and attrition became the critical factors. In this respect the Peace of Versailles of 1783 decided nothing, and the pre-war naval arms race intensified.

CHAPTER SEVEN

Total War:
Britain, France
and the Struggle
for Survival
1793–1802

*Exploiting command of the sea: with no rival
fleets at sea, inshore operations became the
front line. One of the finest exploits of this
type was the cutting out of the French corvette
La Chevrette from Camaret Bay, near Brest, on
the night of 22 July 1801. The British boarded
the ship, overpowered her large crew and then
sailed her out of the bay, reflecting the highest
levels of skill, daring and confidence. (Philip
de Loutherbourg)*

Total War: Britain, France and the Struggle for Survival 1793–1802

THE END OF THE AMERICAN war did not affect the Anglo-Bourbon naval race, which continued until the end of the 1780s. Between 1780 and 1790, France added 50,000 tons of battleships to her fleet, Spain 40,000 tons and Britain 80,000 tons; even Holland managed 50,000 tons. These were impressive figures, driven by commercial rivalry and instructed by war experience. The three major powers built more, and bigger, three-decked ships. British 90- and 100-gun three-deckers were stretched into 98- and 110-gun ships with superior sailing qualities, while France and Spain produced very big ships of 118 and 112 guns respectively. For the first time since the 1690s the Bourbon navies were creating true battle fleets. They also built 80- and 74-gun two-deckers, but dropped the 64-gunner because their main armament of 24-pounder guns was no longer effective. Despite this, 64s continued to feature in the British battle line until the end of the Napoleonic Wars. The French did not adopt the carronade; industrial weakness forced them to rely on inferior bronze howitzers.

The changing doctrine of the Bourbon navies, symbolized by the new three-deckers, and the conversion of the Spanish three-decker *Santissima Trinidad* into a unique four-decker with 130 guns, made their challenge a far more serious threat than the build-up of the 1770s. However, the accumulation of ships by France and Spain could hardly disguise the fundamental weaknesses that would ruin their effort. In essence, French naval policy was schizophrenic. After 1782 France built a battle fleet at enormous cost, well aware that she could not afford to mobilize it, let alone use it in war. It would appear that Vergennes was trying to rebuild French policy around a new relationship of equality with Britain. In 1783 a new base was began at Cherbourg, but work

In their efforts to increase the firepower of their fleet the Spanish added an extra deck to the Santissima Trinidad, *making her a unique four-decked ship with over 130 guns. As one of the largest ships afloat she made an obvious target for British attacks at Cape St Vincent, and at Trafalgar. Her extra guns availed her little as the British gunners fired so much faster.*

was abandoned six years later for lack of money. The Spanish fleet was probably intended to deter both the British and their own American colonists. By 1793 the combined Franco-Spanish fleet was one third larger than the British fleet, and the sheer size of these forces would make it that much more difficult for the British to wear down their opponents in the attritional struggle for command of the sea.

Although she had been defeated in the American war, Britain was not greatly damaged, and after a brief eclipse her European position recovered. In 1787 Prime Minister William Pitt the Younger mobilized the fleet to overthrow the pro-French regime in Holland and drive out French influence. In 1790 the Spanish seizure of the British trading station and shipping at Nootka Sound (Vancouver Island) prompted Pitt to mobilize, forcing the isolated and financially weakened Spanish to back down. Pitt also secured large territorial and trade concessions. Without seamen and money Spain could not resist Britain. The following year Pitt overplayed his hand, relying on naval power to force Russia to disgorge the fortress of Ochakov. Although he mobilized thirty battleships, with a full range of support-craft for Baltic service under Lord Hood, the Russians ignored the threat. Unlike Nootka, which had been a popular commercial issue, Ochakov promised no financial gain and divided the country; Pitt had to back down. Where the Spanish had seen their hollow deterrent exposed, so Pitt had to accept that even British seapower was only an effective political instrument when it was used with the whole weight of the nation behind it.

By 1790 political turmoil had undermined the discipline and subordination of the French service; dockyard workers and seamen were openly defiant of authority, and not above lynching unpopular officers. Lacking support from the government, the officer corps simply melted away. In 1792 the Revolutionary government declared war on Austria in an attempt to reunite the nation. Military failure led to further radicalization, culminating in the execution of the king in January 1793, the French occupation of Belgium, the opening of the River Scheldt to commerce in breach of the 1648 Treaty of Westphalia, and a French declaration of war against Britain on 1 February 1793. For the next twenty-two years British war aims remained remarkably consistent: the expulsion of the French from Belgium. On land, the First Coalition, Britain, Spain, Austria, Prussia, Sardinia and Naples, was demolished by the politicized military power of Revolutionary France, which abandoned the rigid formalism of the 'Age of Reason' for dynamic mass attacks relying on weight of artillery, speed of movement and momentum to sweep aside mechanistically drilled regulars. However, enthusiasm, mass and rhetoric had little value at sea.

When the French fleet was mobilized in 1793 there were few officers, the ships were in disrepair, the dockyards empty and the men mutinous. The revolt of local political interests against the centralizing Jacobins led to the surrender of Toulon and the Mediterranean fleet to the British and Spanish in August. In September the Atlantic fleet mutinied, and order was only restored by a rigorous application of the 'Terror' by Deputy Jeanbon St André, a former merchant captain. Although St André mobilized an impressive force, neither he nor the guillotine could make up for the lack of seamen and experienced officers. Despite these weaknesses, the Republican government planned to invade Britain.

British strategy tried to balance the conflicting demands for a continental military presence with the global strategy of maritime power. The effective use of naval power was complicated by the sheer size of the pre-war French Navy, which made most policy makers cautious. The basis for command of the sea would be the fleet in the Western Approaches, blockading Brest, with another fleet observing Toulon. These blockades would enable Britain to clear the seas of French possessions, French ships and French seafarers. The blockade would also intercept naval stores from the Baltic, weakening the _matériel_ of French seapower. Seizing territory would provide diplomatic counters for peace, and as the French West Indian islands were the most dynamic part of her economy, their loss would damage French finances. Unfortunately this programme would take time to produce any significant effect, and to rulers in Berlin and Vienna it gave the distinct impression that Britain was following her own interests.

In 1793 the French were inactive, so the Grand Fleet assembled slowly at Spithead under Lord Howe. The need to reinforce the Mediterranean and other theatres prevented Howe from getting an adequate force together until the summer, when he undertook a training cruise. After ordering local offensives in the West Indies, the British sent an army to attack Dunkirk. While Pitt wanted to extend the offensive, attacking Brest, Le Havre, Toulon and Mauritius, the shortage of troops led him to support Royalist risings in north-west France. These were quickly crushed by the Republic. The British campaign in the West Indies in 1794 captured most of the French islands, but the human wastage in this theatre made it difficult to hold them.

Since Drake the dream of every British Admiral has been to burn the enemy fleet in its own dockyard. Here Lord Hood retreats from Toulon, leaving much of the French fleet in flames. Inter-allied rivalries prevented a more complete destruction and some ships survived, but only until they encountered his favourite pupil at the Nile. (T. Whitcombe)

The occupation of Toulon by Lord Hood between August and December 1793 was a golden opportunity to destroy a major French fleet and dockyard. However, Anglo-Spanish tensions, local interests and the sudden collapse of the defence ensured that less than half the French fleet was taken or burnt, although large timber piles and mast stores were destroyed. The vengeance of the victorious Jacobins on the town ensured that the French fleet would not be efficient for some years. A scratch fleet was sent to sea from Toulon in the following year, but officers, men and stores were lacking.

In May 1794 the French government sent the Brest fleet 400 miles out into the Atlantic to cover the arrival of an important grain convoy from America. Admiral Villaret-Joyeuse, with St André at his side, encountered Lord Howe, but having no desire to fight, Villaret parried several attempts by the master tactician to bring him to battle.

On 1 June 1794, twenty-six French ships engaged twenty-five British after two days of indecisive skirmishing. Howe's plan was to break through the French from the windward at all points, and then engage from the leeward, which would exploit the superior close-quarters fighting power of the British ships. Howe's direct control and tactical style reflected the limited ability of his own fleet. In the event, few of the British ships managed to get through, Howe's flagship, the *Queen Charlotte*, being the best handled. As she passed under the stern of Villaret's *Montagne* and across the bows of the *Jacobin*, she fought both broadsides, a rare feat, and shattered both ships. Despite the failure of his drill- ground ambitions, Howe's attack ruptured the French line, creating a mêlée. Villaret found part of his fleet closely engaged, most being too crippled to escape, while the others lay to leeward and were trying to return. Running down to this disengaged body, Villaret regained control and beat back into action to rescue some of the disabled ships. Howe had a similar problem, and his flagship was partly disabled. Villaret rescued four or five ships, but had to leave six others as prizes, while the *Vengeur du Peuple* sank after a vicious battle with the *Brunswick*, fought out with the two ships grinding against

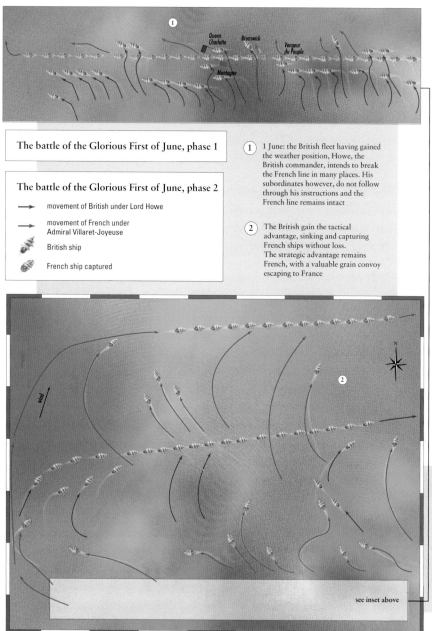

The battle of the Glorious First of June, phase 1

The battle of the Glorious First of June, phase 2

→ movement of British under Lord Howe

→ movement of French under Admiral Villaret-Joyeuse

🚢 British ship

🚢 French ship captured

(1) 1 June: the British fleet having gained the weather position, Howe, the British commander, intends to break the French line in many places. His subordinates however, do not follow through his instructions and the French line remains intact

(2) The British gain the tactical advantage, sinking and capturing French ships without loss. The strategic advantage remains French, with a valuable grain convoy escaping to France

see inset above

Although short of seamanship and fleet experience the French ships at the Glorious First fought with rare determination. Here HMS Brunswick *engages the* Vengeur, *hooked into her starboard anchors, and the* Achille, *which has just lost the last of her masts. The* Vengeur *sank, and the* Achille *was taken. (Philip de Loutherbourg)*

each other. Howe's victory, celebrated as the 'Glorious First of June' for want of a nearby land feature to give it a name, reasserted the Royal Navy's mastery in battle.

Having won a great victory after four days in sight of the enemy, Howe, now 68 years old, was simply too tired to carry on. Unfortunately he was badly served by his staff, who allowed the French to get away with their crippled ships and failed to intercept the 117-ship convoy, depriving Howe of the strategic fruits of his tactical success.

The battle of the Glorious First of June

Despite a lifetime of experience Lord Howe planned a perfect battle, in which his fleet would break through the French line at all points, engage from the leeward to prevent the enemy from escaping.In the event many of his captains failed to execute their orders and, although the resulting chaos enabled superior British ship-handling and gunnery to triumph, only seven French ships were taken or sunk.

In 1794 Lord Hood's Mediterranean fleet liberated Corsica, Captain Horatio Nelson (1758–1805) losing the sight of one eye while serving ashore. In 1795 the French Mediterranean fleet was defeated by the British under Admiral Hotham, in two battles notable for the insight, initiative and courage shown by Nelson.

In the Atlantic Villaret attempted to cut off a small detachment of five British battleships, but Admiral Sir William Cornwallis in the *Royal Sovereign* conducted a masterly fighting retreat. A few days later Villaret lost three battleships to Lord Bridport off Île de Groix, and was pinned down at Lorient, powerless to stop Royalist forces landing at Quiberon. However, General Hoche crushed the rising and then attempted to invade Ireland. Although they evaded Bridport's distant blockade, the French ships were scattered by storms and the attempt failed.

The French conquered Holland in 1795, taking control of the Dutch fleet. The British responded by capturing the Dutch bases at the Cape of Good Hope and Ceylon. In late 1796 Spain changed sides, reversing the naval balance at a stroke. The British fleet, now heavily outnumbered, evacuated the Mediterranean and fell back on Lisbon. The new allies decided to combine their main fleets.

When Admiral de Cordoba's fleet of twenty-seven ships sailed for Brest it was intercepted off Cape St Vincent by fifteen British ships, commanded by Admiral Sir John Jervis (1735–1823) in HMS *Victory* on 14 February 1797. The Spanish were driven back into Cádiz in disorder, having lost four ships and suffered heavy casualties. The battle turned on the initiative of Nelson, who took his ship out of the line to engage the enemy in anticipation of Jervis's wishes. By his action Nelson, supported by his friends Cuthbert Collingwood and Thomas Troubridge, prevented the scattered Spanish force from regrouping. With his ship crippled, Nelson ran her alongside the Spanish 74-gun *San Nicolas*, which he took by boarding, before moving on to board the even larger 112-gun three-decker *San Josef,* which had run foul of her in the confusion.

After the battle Jervis, now Earl St Vincent, blockaded Cádiz and detached Nelson to intercept a silver fleet, apparently at Tenerife. There was no silver fleet and Nelson lost his right arm in a night boat attack.

Between April and August 1797 the British Grand Fleet based at Spithead, and the North Sea Fleet based at the Nore, mutinied over pay and conditions of service afloat. The grievances of the men were clear, and the government unwisely resisted, provoking the reluctant men to mutiny. At Spithead good order and sense prevailed: the fleet was ready to go to sea if the French came out, and frigates remained off Brest. Eventually, Lord Howe returned from sick leave to negotiate a settlement. Pay and conditions were improved and the men pardoned. The Nore mutiny was an altogether more sinister event, closely connected to republican political groups, and several of the ringleaders were executed after it collapsed. Even so, the underlying good order of the Nore fleet received a powerful restatement in the autumn.

When Admiral de Winter's sixteen Dutch battleships were deployed to support another attempted invasion of Ireland, they were intercepted off Camperdown on 11 October 1797 by Admiral Sir Adam (later Earl) Duncan leading the Nore fleet of the same nominal force. In the failing light, and close to shoal waters that would enable the Dutch to escape, Duncan abandoned his attempt to form a line of battle and ordered his fleet to engage. The British came down on the wind in two roughly formed columns, smashing through the Dutch line before settling the battle with superior firepower at close quarters. As usual in Anglo-Dutch sea fights this was a costly affair: nine Dutch ships were taken, including de Winter's flagship. The survivors escaped, but the invasion was abandoned. In August 1799 an Anglo-Russian landing at Den Helder captured most of the remaining seaworthy Dutch battleships.

In the Mediterranean St Vincent's iron will crushed the first signs of mutiny. He ordered the execution of two mutineers, hauled up to the yard arm by their shipmates, on Easter Sunday. The lesson was critical, because St Vincent's fleet would be called upon to complete the victories of 1797. In May 1798 Napoleon Bonaparte, conqueror of Italy and among the most powerful men in France, launched an invasion of Egypt with 36,000 men aboard 400 transports, a dozen battleships and

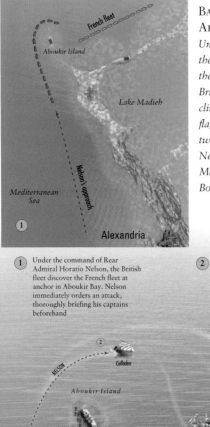

Aboukir Island

French fleet

Lake Madieh

Mediterranean Sea

Nelson's approach

Alexandria

1

BATTLE OF THE NILE: ABOUKIR BAY

Unable to support the ships at the head of their line, the wind being directly against, the French were destroyed in detail, with British ships firing from both sides. The climax came after dark, when the French flagship L'Orient *blew up. The next day two French ships escaped. In one battle Nelson had recovered command of the Mediterranean, and destroyed Bonaparte's dream of eastern empire.*

1 Under the command of Rear Admiral Horatio Nelson, the British fleet discover the French fleet at anchor in Aboukir Bay. Nelson immediately orders an attack, thoroughly briefing his captains beforehand

2 The four leading British ships make their way inshore of the French line, risking shoals and shallow water. The British main body attacks the seaward

NELSON

2

Culloden

Aboukir Island

Vanguard

wind

Damaged frigate

S h a l l o w s

Batteries

other warships. Bonaparte seized Malta from the Knights of St John before pressing on to Alexandria. Although this expedition had been the talk of Europe, the destination remained unknown. The British government ordered St Vincent to send the convalescent Nelson with a small detachment to watch the French. Just before Bonaparte left Toulon, a gale blew Nelson off station, dismasting his flagship and sending his frigates back to Gibraltar. When further intelligence arrived from London, Nelson was reinforced with ten battleships, the cream of St Vincent's fleet. After a relentless pursuit which saw him miss the French for want of frigates and reach Alexandria the day before Bonaparte, Nelson finally located the French battle fleet in Aboukir Bay late on the afternoon of 1 August 1798.

3 During the night the French flagship L'Orient is set on fire. As the fire reaches her powder magazine she blows up, scattering wreckage over a wide distance

4 The dawn reveals a complete victory for Nelson, with nine enemy ships captured and two sunk. Only four French ships under Admiral Villeneuve escape. The victory is so complete that the British are confirmed as the dominant naval power in the Mediterranean. Meanwhile Napoleon's army is left in Egypt without naval support or supplies

8 pm: Swiftsure
Alexander
Bellerophon
Majestic
L'Orient sunk
Tonnant
Sunk

Battle of the Nile, Aboukir Bay
1–2 August 1798

- - ➤ British under Nelson

- - ➤ French under Brueys

Without a moment's hesitation Nelson ordered an attack. He relied on the tactical ideas he had discussed with his captains and their professional expertise to secure a victory. His confidence was not misplaced. As HMS *Goliath* led the fleet into the bay, Captain Foley, who had a current atlas, could see the French ships were at single anchor. This meant there had to be room for them to swing with the tide, and so he could go inside their line. This tactic had not been anticipated by Admiral Brueys, who fancied his position was strong, and expected an attack on the rear of his line, where he had concentrated his most powerful ships. When the British appeared he expected they would wait until the morning. With the wind blowing down the French line from head to stern, it was impossible for the rear ships to come up to support the van. During the approach Troubridge's ship went aground on a shoal, warning the others to keep clear. Foley took his ship inside the leading French ship, devastating *Guerrier* before she could clear her port batteries for action. The next four ships followed Foley, and when Nelson took his flagship outside their line, the French ships were exposed to devastating fire from superior gun crews on both sides. The first three ships in the French line were quickly demolished. Only the huge 120-gun *L'Orient* had the power to beat off her attacker, the *Bellerophon*, but her fate was sealed by a fire among paint pots on deck. When *L'Orient* blew up at 10 p.m. the firing ceased for ten to fifteen minutes, with men on both sides stunned by the noise, awestruck and horrified by the spectacle. Then the British began firing again. By midnight only three French battleships had not surrendered. At this point the battle came to a standstill from sheer exhaustion, the British gun crews dropping asleep beside their cannon, while Nelson, who had been struck on the forehead by a jagged piece of iron and concussed, was unable to maintain the battle. In the morning two French battleships, led by Rear Admiral Villeneuve, escaped, the

Finding the enemy fleet at anchor late in the afternoon Nelson immediately launched an attack. On board the leading ship, HMS Goliath, Captain Foley realized he could run inside the French line, doubling the attack. Foley knew Nelson would approve his initiative, and exploit it. (Nicholas Pocock)

British being too disabled to pursue; the third ran aground and was burnt. Nine French battleships had been taken, and two destroyed.

In a letter to Lord Howe, Nelson generously attributed his success at the battle of the Nile to his captains, calling them his 'band of brothers'. It was another sign of his superior mind that although he belonged to Lord Hood's more permissive school of tactics, Nelson acknowledged Howe as the leading officer in the service, and praised the contribution that his signalling system had made to tactical control. The failure to burn the French fleet at Toulon in 1793, or to destroy it at sea in 1795, had been rectified. Nelson had made the Mediterranean a British lake, imprisoning Bonaparte in Egypt, and providing a focus for the creation of a second coalition by Britain, Austria and Russia, with Naples, Turkey and Portugal. Having discovered that a maritime war with limited continental involvement would not work, Britain tried to create a grand alliance to overthrow France, but the Second Coalition lacked the necessary unity of purpose to do this. Nelson had achieved all that seapower could, and rather more, but victory at sea alone would not defeat France.

The fruits of victory. Nelson took his fleet from Aboukir Bay to the Bay of Naples, where he persuaded the king to join the war against France. Soon afterwards Captain Thomas Troubridge would lead a Neapolitan army into Rome. Later the French conquered Naples, forcing the king, Nelson and Lady Hamilton back to Sicily.

After the Nile Nelson left a force to blockade Egypt and went to Naples, where he persuaded the king to join the war. Within weeks Troubridge, at the head of the Neapolitan army, had captured Rome. Unfortunately the Neapolitan troops then collapsed and Nelson had to evacuate the king to Sicily. After a popular uprising Nelson restored royal authority in Naples, but he was recalled to England because of insubordination and his interference in local politics.

Although trapped in Egypt, Bonaparte resumed his campaign in early 1799, marching north to invest the crusader fortress of Acre. Captain Sidney Smith's squadron captured his siege train, which had been sent by sea, and landed it with naval gunners, a reinforcement that enabled the Turkish garrison to drive off the French. Bonaparte left Egypt on 22 August, and established himself as First Consul of France and effective dictator in November. The French troops in Malta and Egypt capitulated in 1800 and 1801. When St Vincent took command of the Channel fleet in 1799 he imposed a close blockade that kept the French pinned in harbour, cut their supplies and provided the basis for success in a total war.

The Second Coalition did not outlast the first flush of victory, for France, galvanized by Bonaparte, resumed the war with vigour, while Austria and Russia quarrelled. Russia soon left the war, and Austria finally admitted defeat in early 1801. In December 1800 the Scandinavian powers, led by Tsar Paul and aided by France, formed the 'Armed Neutrality of the North' to impose on Britain a liberal interpretation of belligerent rights at sea. As an opening gambit Paul seized the British merchant ships in his harbours. Once again alone in her war with France, Britain acted energetically, sending a powerful fleet to the Baltic under Admiral Hyde Parker, with Nelson as second in command.

On 2 April 1801 Nelson attacked the floating defences of Copenhagen with twelve small battleships, frigates and mortar vessels. The battle was a straightforward artillery contest. By 1 p.m. three British ships had drifted out of the line, and another had gone aground before getting into the battle. At this point Parker made a permissive signal to disengage, well aware that his second would never give up without orders, but leaving the final decision with Nelson. Nelson famously remarked that he did not see the signal, having put his telescope to his blind eye. Two hours later he offered the Danes an armistice to remove their wounded from the floating batteries and hulks that had surrendered. This provided the crown prince with an opportunity to end the bloodshed, and Denmark left the Armed Neutrality.

Over 2,000 men had died to prove the point that second-rank powers had no business challenging the belligerent rights of great powers engaged in a struggle for survival. Seapower might have limits, but it remained an awesome instrument in the hands of resolute politicians and brilliant admirals. Parker was recalled and Nelson planned to attack the Russian fleet at Reval, but after the murder of Tsar Paul the Russians backed down.

The battle of Copenhagen, 2 April 1801. With his talent for finding the key position Nelson used his fleet to defeat the Danish floating defences, so that his bomb vessels, seen in the left foreground, could be brought up to bombard the city. Most accounts of the battle concentrate on the hard fighting, ignoring the operational thinking that guided it. Nelson never fought for the sake of fighting, only to secure real objectives. (Nicholas Pocock)

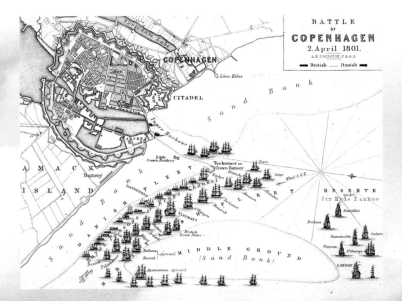

*Nelson quickly spotted the flaw in the Danish defences, the lack of a fortress in the
deep water channel off the city which left it open to mortar bombardment. The
Danes had built a battery there in the eighteenth century, but did not maintain it.
They would build another after 1801, forcing the second British attack to adopt a
different approach.*

In 1801 Bonaparte built invasion craft at Boulogne to put pressure on the British to make the peace he could not secure by force. Nelson attacked the flotilla in August, but found them too well defended. Although an Anglo-French peace was signed at Amiens in March 1802, the terms, essentially the return of non-European possessions, reflected British war-weariness, and a hope that the new French regime might be stable. The failure to remove the French from Belgium and Holland ensured that the settlement could only be a truce. Once again, the bulk of France's maritime population had ended up in British prisons, some 70,000 men by 1801. By contrast Britain was literally able to 'harvest the sea', taking on sailors from every possible source, ranging from native-born volunteers to released slaves, enemy nationals and neutral sailors.

By surviving, and posing a threat to Britain, the French Navy had served the Republic well, despite being short of men and starved of praise. It demonstrated just how difficult it was to make naval power truly effective against continental rivals. The great strategic issue remaining to be settled when the war resumed, only months later, was how to decide the struggle between the land and the sea.

The French empire in Egypt ended when General Abercromby's army stormed ashore at Aboukir on 8 March 1801. This brilliant amphibious assault operation drove the French off the beach, and was followed by a comprehensive victory on 21 March. The landing demonstrated British mastery of power projection, and the strategic flexibility provided by sea control. (Philip de Loutherbourg)

CHAPTER EIGHT

Seapower and Landpower: the Napoleonic Wars 1803–15

Britannia's God of War, Horatio, Lord Nelson.
Nelson combined the dedication and experience
of a career professional with the insight of
genius, humanity and unmatched moral
courage. Although there were several fine fleet
commanders among his contemporaries, none
could match the inspired simplicity of his
tactics, or the overpowering presence of his
leadership. (Lemuel Abbott)

Seapower and Landpower:
the Napoleonic Wars 1803–15

NAPOLEON TREATED THE PEACE OF AMIENS as an opportunity to reconstruct Italy, create tariff barriers against British trade, and retain Holland and Belgium. He expected the truce would last at least four years, giving him time to rebuild his fleet, recover the French colonies and develop trade. However, his contempt for the 'nation of shopkeepers' proved misplaced. In 1803 the British refused to evacuate Malta and declared war. By seizing the initiative they swept up much of the French mercantile marine, along with several warships. From the first day of the war naval attrition was rapidly reducing French options.

Taken by surprise, Napoleon renewed his attempt to create an invasion flotilla capable of transporting an army of 100,000 men across the Channel. While the small craft were soon built, France lacked the naval power to convoy such a cumbersome force. Furthermore, the British were quick to respond. A sustained coastal offensive, largely conducted by gunboats and mortar vessels, forced the invasion craft into a few heavily defended harbours around Boulogne, where the 'army of England' was encamped. These harbours were so small that the flotilla could not get to sea in less than three high tides – a full twenty-four hours – which would give the British ample opportunity to intercept. The British also pioneered new weapons to attack Boulogne, such as Robert Fulton's floating mines and William Congreve's war rockets.

Recognizing that Spain was actively assisting France, the British captured the Spanish treasure fleet, crippling Spanish finances and bringing her into the war. With the addition of the Spanish fleet, Napoleon saw a new opportunity to invade. However, he had a complex problem to solve. At the outbreak of war the First Lord of the Admiralty, Earl St Vincent, had selected the outstanding admirals of the age to command his main fleets. Sir William Cornwallis took the Channel fleet, imposing a close blockade on Brest with detached squadrons covering Rochefort and the other French Atlantic bases. St Vincent knew that whatever the odds against him, Cornwallis would not be defeated. On him rested the whole strategy of the British war effort. So long as France could not control the Channel, Britain and her empire were safe. Cornwallis's fleet included almost all the three-decked ships. St Vincent realized that Nelson's unique genius was ill-suited to the static, primarily defensive task given to Cornwallis, and sent him to the Mediterranean, relying on him to pursue and destroy any French fleet that left Toulon. Consequently, while Cornwallis kept close to Brest, leaving the French in no doubt that he would engage them if they left the roadstead, Nelson often fell back from Toulon, trying to draw the French out. Such an open blockade, as 1793–9 had shown, was too risky for the Channel.

If he wanted to invade Britain Napoleon would have to break down this well-organized, doctrinally coherent system with fleets based at Toulon, Cartagena, Cádiz, Ferrol, Rochefort and Brest. On land, Napoleon relied on combining separate forces on the field, using speed to outmanoeuvre his enemies and bring them to battle, when mass attacks would destroy them. Yet his naval planning displayed all the faults to be found in the French campaign of 1759, and ended in a very similar way. He tried to outwit the British and avoid battle. This ran against his own practice, and ignored the communication difficulties inherent in naval operations before the wireless.

As forces became available Napoleon altered his plans. The invasion flotilla was largely complete by late 1804, while a Spanish battle fleet was promised for March 1805. He ordered the Rochefort and Toulon squadrons to sea in January 1805, to stage diversionary operations in the West Indies. He hoped these movements would enable the main fleet at Brest to get into the Channel. The Rochefort squadron completed its mission, but Admiral Villeneuve's fleet put back to Toulon after storm damage. A second plan expected Admiral Ganteaume to get out of Brest without a fight and rendezvous in the West Indies with the Toulon and Rochefort fleets, reinforced by the

Spanish ships from Ferrol and Cádiz, before putting back for the Channel. This plan was stifled by Cornwallis's close watch. However, Villeneuve finally got to sea at the end of March with eleven battleships, picked up six more at Cádiz, and reached the West Indies in May. By this time Nelson was hot on his heels with a smaller force. On his arrival Villeneuve was reinforced by three ships, and told that unless Ganteaume appeared he was to return to Ferrol for reinforcements, before opening the blockade of Brest. Nelson arrived in early June, after a much faster crossing; he picked up the local squadron and sought the French. Villeneuve sailed for Ferrol on 9 June. Once Nelson knew this he sailed for Gibraltar on 13 June, sending a fast brig to England. The brig passed Villeneuve's fleet, noted its course, and reported it to the Admiralty on 8 July. Admiral Lord Barham, the elderly First Lord, rapidly reorganized his forces, and dispatched orders to counter the French. Recognizing that their landfall would be Cape Finisterre (Spain), he ordered Admiral Sir Robert Calder to raise the blockade of Ferrol, and rendezvous there with ships from off Rochefort and elements of the Channel fleet. On 22 July, in thick weather, Calder met Villeneuve. Although he had only fifteen battleships against twenty, Calder attacked the allied rear, hoping to cut it off. In poor visibility, caused by gunsmoke and fog, any tactical finesse was lost. Ships could hardly see their next head, and rather less of their opponents. Two Spanish ships were taken. The following day, when Calder realized the allies still outnumbered him, he chose not to renew the action. He did not share Nelson's relentless drive to annihilate the enemy, or his view that it was his duty to continue the action for as long as he could, to cripple the allied invasion plans. For this he would be criticized and effectively disgraced.

Villeneuve saw no reason to renew the battle, and put in to Vigo. Napoleon was astonished by the speed of the British reaction, apparently unaware that the landfall of his fleet could have been predicted. Villeneuve was ordered to join the Rochefort squadron and sail for Brest, but a subsidiary clause allowed him to go to Cádiz for

Spanish reinforcements if necessary. Villeneuve, already demoralized, lacked the will to try his luck. When he put to sea on 10 August 1805, he saw that the frigate sent to pick up the Rochefort squadron was already a British prize, and convinced himself that twenty-five British battleships were just over the horizon. On the 14th he turned south. Although the Rochefort squadron of five battleships was at sea, it could not find Villeneuve.

At Brest Ganteaume moved his fleet into the outer anchorage on 22 August, but Cornwallis, desperate for a battle, immediately ran in to engage and drove them back under the cover of the land batteries. Realizing his plans had collapsed, Napoleon put the Grande Armée in motion for the Austrian frontier, and mothballed his flotilla. As he could not get to grips with the British he would settle accounts with Austria and Russia. Villeneuve was ordered to land troops in Sicily. His fleet had been demoted from a principal actor to a bit part player. At Cádiz Villeneuve and the Spanish Admiral Gravina refitted their fleets and mobilized more Spanish ships, but they were short of naval stores and food, while the crews were sickly and inexperienced. When Villeneuve arrived off Cádiz Admiral Collingwood, with only three ships, stood aside, but by 28 September Calder and Nelson, restored by a brief spell ashore, had joined. The fleets were roughly equal, thirty-three battleships each, but mere numbers told only half the story. Nelson knew the allied ships were inefficient and rated them as only half as good as equivalent British units. Desperate for a battle, he pressed the blockade, hoping to starve the allies out, although his own logistics required divisions to be sent away for food and water. When Admiral Louis took his ships to the Moroccan coast, and Calder went home in his flagship, there were only twenty-seven British ships off Cádiz. Villeneuve put to sea on 20 October. Late that day Nelson came into visual contact, and Villeneuve formed a line with the allied ships intermixed. He later changed course, heading north towards Cádiz. With the wind light and a heavy swell setting in, the allied line was imperfectly formed, being bowed away to the east, bunched and in places overlapping. Villeneuve was under no illusions about what would happen. He knew the British would use dynamic, aggressive tactics, exploiting their superior doctrine, experience and seamanship to destroy the cohesion of his line. If Villeneuve was despondent he had good reason: he had been at the Nile.

Nelson's captains had all been personally briefed over dinner in the great cabin of the *Victory*. He would attack in two columns: one was to cut the allied line about midway along, the other to destroy the allied rear, while the first prevented the allied van from interfering. The object was annihilation, and Nelson expected to take at least twenty of the enemy. Nelson led the centre column in *Victory*, supported by two more three-deckers, the 'Fighting' *Temeraire* and the *Neptune*. Collingwood led the second column, with his flag in the 100-gun *Royal*

The enduring legacy of Trafalgar, a print from The Boy's Own Paper *of 1885 showing the famous signal, and the number of each hoist in the signal book. By this time Nelson, the battle and his flagship had become a central element in the national self-image, and the naval tradition. (Walter May)*

Sovereign. Each captain knew the object of the attack, and was advised to look to his own line and his squadron commander for guidance. A final catch-all was provided in the *Trafalgar Memorandum* of 9 October 1805: 'But in case signals can neither be seen nor perfectly understood, no Captain can do very wrong if he places his ship alongside that of the enemy.' This was intended to guide officers more noted for courage than insight. Nelson would not attempt to direct the fleet once the fighting started: there was no need to interfere with his veterans as they carried out their mission within the broad instructions he had provided. The contrast with Lord Rodney in 1780, unable to make himself understood by captains he had not troubled to invite to dine, let alone to discuss his ideas, was complete.

On the morning of 21 October 1805 the fleets were in sight, but the wind was light and the closing speed was a little under two miles an hour. This gave the men time for breakfast and lunch. The effect of this prolonged period of visual contact on morale cannot be overestimated. For the British, it held out the expectation of crushing victory, spiced by personal danger; for the allies there could be little doubt that they would be defeated, and many of them would be killed. Despite the psychological pressures the allies would fight with courage. Their problem was the truly exceptional nature of the enemy. Just as Napoleon crushed outdated, ill-organized and tactically inflexible forces on land, Nelson would annihilate the outclassed Franco-Spanish navies at sea.

The British approached in no particular order, ships struggling to get into line, gradually settling into two columns. This formation sacrificed firepower for speed. Nelson knew there would be a storm that night, foretold by the barometer in his cabin and a heavy swell, and he was anxious to secure a decision that day. While the bows of wooden warships designed for linear combat were low, lightweight structures which offered little protection from heavy shot, Nelson was confident that the allies would not be able to stop his attack.

At 10 a.m. Collingwood ordered his column to open out into a line of bearing, each ship picking a point in the allied line where they would break through. Nelson kept his column in formation, needing to concentrate his mass at the critical point, and manoeuvring to disguise the point of impact. However, he was always going to seek out the allied commander. The famous signal 'England expects that every man will do his duty' revealed his human side. He appreciated the morale value of the gesture, and

THE BATTLE OF TRAFALGAR, 21 OCTOBER 1805

Nelson's tactics at Trafalgar were designed to force a close quarters mêlée battle on an enemy he knew to be inferior in ship-handling and firepower. He took a huge risk, approaching bow on in two columns to speed up the process, and ensure the fighting was over by sunset, as he anticipated a storm. His own formation broke the allied line, cutting off the after two thirds of the fleet to be overwhelmed by Collingwood's division, while the leading third were held off. It had the great quality of simplicity, and worked as intended.

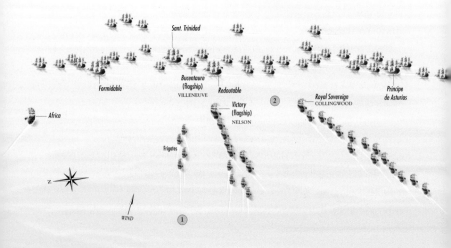

Battle of Trafalgar
21 October 1805

(1) 21 October, morning: Admiral Nelson orders his captains to approach the enemy line in two columns, the left led by himself and the right led by Admiral Collingwood

(2) Midday: the British fleet approaches the Franco-Spanish line, the strongest British ships placed in the lead. They take heavy punishment before being able to penetrate the enemy line and bring their own broadsides to bear

Sant. Trinidad

Formidable

Bucentaure (flagship)
VILLENEUVE

Redoutable

Royal Sovereign
COLLINGWOOD

Principe de Asturias

Africa

Victory (flagship)
NELSON

Frigates

W-E

WIND

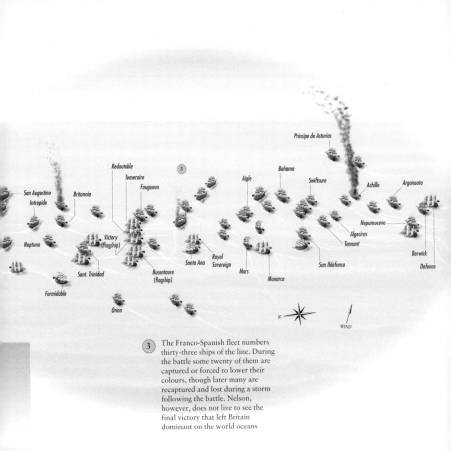

3 The Franco-Spanish fleet numbers thirty-three ships of the line. During the battle some twenty of them are captured or forced to lower their colours, though later many are recaptured and lost during a storm following the battle. Nelson, however, does not live to see the final victory that left Britain dominant on the world oceans

although Collingwood wondered why he had bothered, the men cheered, greatly encouraged by this personal message from their beloved admiral. The signal was flown at 11.56 a.m. At 12.00 he hoisted 'Prepare to anchor after the close of day', and at 12.20, shortly before going into action, 'Engage the enemy more closely'. The signals were left flying throughout the battle.

The firing began at midday, when the *Royal Sovereign* came within range. Collingwood's flagship broke through the allied line astern of the 112-gun *Santa Anna*, which received a shattering broadside through her lightly built stern galleries, and was then closely engaged on the leeward side. *Royal Sovereign* was soon surrounded by allied ships and was effectively dismasted before her supporters came into action.

Victory ran down the allied line from the north, exchanging fire with several ships before pushing under the stern of Villeneuve's flagship, the 84-gun *Bucentaure*, at approximately 12.30. A raking broadside of double-loaded guns, beginning with a 68-pounder carronade loaded with shot and a barrel of musket balls, mowed down everything in its path, effectively clearing *Bucentaure*'s gun decks. Unable to break through, being blocked by the 74-gun *Redoutable*, *Victory* ran into her new opponent, and her momentum drove the two ships through the

line, opening the way for the *Temeraire*. *Redoutable*'s crew had been trained to clear the enemy upper deck with musketry and board. At 1.30 p.m. one of the marksmen aloft shot and mortally wounded Nelson as he walked on the upper deck in full uniform. Just as Captain Lucas prepared to board, having abandoned his guns, the *Temeraire* came alongside and annihilated his crew with a single broadside. At 3.30 p.m. the shattered *Redoutable* had surrendered. The fighting around *Victory*, *Bucentaure* and the Spanish four-decker *Santissima*

Trafalgar, with HMS Victory at the heart of the fighting. By leading the attack Nelson set an example to his fleet, and ensured there could be no mistake as to his purpose. He weighted the head of his column with three three-decked ships, for maximum impact. (Clarkson Stansfield)

Trinidad was now the core of the battle. While Collingwood's ships came up and completed the work begun by their admiral, Nelson's supporters had to ensure that the van of the allied line, commanded by Admiral Dumanoir, did not get back into the fighting. Villeneuve had ordered him to get into action as quickly as possible, but light winds and irresolution hampered his efforts. After using boats to tow the heads of his four ships round, Dumanoir was driven off. (His four ships were captured on 2 November, off Cape Finisterre.) Shortly after that *Bucentaure* and *Santissima Trinidad* surrendered.

All this time Nelson lay in the cockpit of *Victory*, paralysed by the musket ball which had smashed through his left lung before lodging in his spine, and slowly drowning in his own blood. Aware that he had won a great victory, he died at 4.30 p.m., just as Villeneuve's flag came down. His death overshadowed the British triumph.

The battle gradually died away: the French *Achille* blew up at 5.30 p.m., and a few allied ships managed to creep away, but seventeen had surrendered. Collingwood did not anchor, and lost many of the prizes in the gale that followed the battle. The allies had fought with courage and determination; only two captains were censured, while the crews of both nations performed far better than they had done in the previous war. Yet the fundamental truth remained that the British were professionals, and the allies brave but inexperienced amateurs. The rate of fire from the British ships was at least double that of the allies, their ship-handling was superior, their tactical insight and understanding on an altogether higher plane. Nelson led a fleet of veterans, bound together by common doctrine and supreme confidence. Few of them had served with Nelson before the campaign, and some, like Edward Codrington of the 74-gun *Orion*, only met him off Cádiz. Yet despite Codrington's initial scepticism, he quickly fell under Nelson's spell. He was proud to paint his ship in 'Nelson fashion', with black bands on each gun deck, as seen on the *Victory* to this day. This helped recognition in the mêlée, when the smoke and confusion could result in 'friendly fire'. Nelson won the battle at close quarters: having broken up the allied line he achieved a decisive concentration of force. This 'concentration' was not numerical – there were fewer British ships fighting than allied units throughout the decisive phase of the battle – it was simply a matter of getting to close range, where rapid fire was decisive. The British lost 250 killed and 1,200 wounded. The allied casualties, bearing in mind the loss of several ships in the gale, were at least 5,000. *Redoutable* alone had 578 killed and wounded from a crew of 672, *Bucentaure* fared little better. After being released Villeneuve, a broken and demoralized man, went back to France where some believe he committed suicide.

With the death of Nelson, the greatest of all naval commanders, and the first British national hero, much of the glory departed from war at sea. Subsequent events paled by comparison with his achievements. Other admirals of the age, for all their solid professionalism, lacked his genius. He should be remembered for his leadership, tactical insight, capacity for decision, resolution, strategic grasp, consummate seamanship, moral courage and humanity.

After Trafalgar the blockade of Brest, for so long maintained at the highest pitch, relaxed. Two squadrons escaped in December, intent on commerce raiding. One was destroyed off San Domingo in February 1806. The other lasted longer, and some of the ships made it home. However, this strategy proved no more successful than the invasion plan. The British were everywhere and the French could only use the sea as fugitives. Several small forces went out, but few achieved their mission before they were taken, burnt or wrecked.

Trafalgar was the last great fleet action under sail. After this the character of war at sea changed. From now on the major operations would be conducted *from* the sea, not *at* sea. While seapower reached new heights, exploiting Nelson's triumph to play a critical role in the overthrow of Napoleon, it was dominated by the economic struggle between Britain and France. The destruction of the Third Coalition at Austerlitz, the annihilation of Prussia at Jena in 1806 and the Franco-Russian accord at Tilsit on 25 June 1807 left Britain completely isolated. To meet the French challenge which threatened her very survival, Britain adopted a global maritime strategy with uncompromising singleness of purpose.

The British recaptured the Cape of Good Hope, and took Curaçao, Buenos Aires and Montevideo, the last two temporarily. These moves were in part an attempt to find new markets for British exports. In the Berlin Decrees of November 1806, which followed the annihilation of Prussia, Napoleon barred British trade from the Continent. His object was to destroy the British economy, the basis of her ability to resist. The British imposed a counter-blockade, the 'Orders in Council', in January and November 1807. These began by prohibiting neutral ships, predominantly American, from trading between two French ports, but went on to demand that any neutral ship carrying cargo to France would have to stop in Britain, unload and purchase a special licence. In effect, all continental ports controlled by the French were blockaded. Napoleon responded with the Milan Decrees of November and December 1807, which extended the blockade to cover neutral ships that had docked at British ports, or even submitted to the British 'Orders'. Once again he miscalculated. The British economy would weather the storm better than the French.

From 1807 Napoleon complemented this economic strategy with a massive programme to build battleships all round his empire, from Hamburg and Den Helder to Venice, by way of Amsterdam, Antwerp, Flushing, the French bases, Genoa, Naples and Venice. By 1812 this continental effort had produced an impressive force, but the impression did not go much beyond the paper on which the ships were listed. Large battleships were of little moment when France, even with her satellites, could not raise and retain anywhere near enough seamen. Crews were filled out with conscripts from every part of Europe, although the Dutch ships were well manned and the Danish volunteers were excellent. The fleet could never have gone to sea. Furthermore, rapid construction ensured that many ships were rotten before they were launched. Eventually, the military needs of the French regime took priority. After his defeat in Russia Napoleon conscripted skilled dockyard workers and seamen into the army. His fleet may well have been a gigantic bluff. Yet, by its very existence it sustained the invasion fears of the British, diverting resources away from offensive strategies.

After Trafalgar the British fleet, so assiduously built up between 1783 and 1793 was over age and worn out. Consequently, Britain replaced 50,000 tons of battleships between 1805 and 1815. New 120-gun first rates were built, combining massive firepower with superior sailing qualities, but the second rate three-decker, the defensive core of British seapower for 150 years, was abandoned. There was no need to think about avoiding defeat; in future the critical objective would be to catch the enemy. Once again, ship design changed to reflect new strategic circumstances. To man this fleet, approximately 100 battleships and 700 other vessels, 145,000 men were serving afloat in 1812 at the height of the maritime war.

In mid August 1807, only seven weeks after Tilsit, 30,000 British troops were landed on the Danish island of Zealand. They bombarded Copenhagen, and then removed every Danish ship that would float,

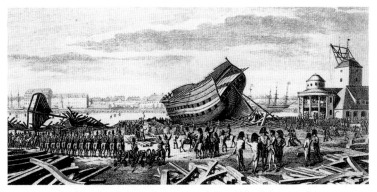

In 1807 the British went back to Copenhagen and, unable to repeat Nelson's bombardment, landed an army and forced the neutral Danes to surrender their fleet, together with the contents of the dockyard. Anything that could not be moved, like these two ships, was destroyed before the British departed. For the next seven years the Danes waged a bitter guerrilla war against British shipping in the Baltic narrows.

and every item of use or value from the dockyard. Fifteen battleships and many smaller vessels were sent to Britain, and what little remained was put to the torch. An entire navy had been destroyed to keep it out of the hands of the French. Although the opposition at home considered the attack immoral, it was decisive. Copenhagen made the world aware that Britain would go to any lengths to survive. At the end of November the Portuguese Navy and their royal family left for Brazil under British escort, just as a French army reached the outskirts of Lisbon. Admiral Sinavin's Russian battle squadron, recently anchored in the Tagus, was blockaded and the crews sent home. Only an attempt to coerce Turkey in 1807 failed: the fleet reached the Sea of Marmora, but the Turks were not impressed.

When French forces did get to sea they were pursued relentlessly. In April 1809 eight battleships left Brest for Rochefort. Although securely

anchored in the Aix Roads, protected by treacherous navigation, floating barriers and local land defences, they were attacked by Captain Lord Cochrane. French defences proved no match for Cochrane's ingenuity, determination and confidence. Already famous for a brilliant amphibious campaign on the east coast of Spain, Cochrane used fireships, rocket boats and explosion vessels to force his way into the roadstead. Despite the lukewarm support of his admiral, Cochrane drove the French out of their anchorage in confusion, and burnt several grounded battleships. With better support the entire fleet could have been destroyed.

In August 1809 the British launched the largest amphibious operation of the war, a bold attempt to capture the French dockyard at Antwerp, and destroy the fleet it contained. A British army of 45,000 men and 450 horses required 352 transports, supported by 40

Lord Cochrane in HMS Imperieuse *leading the attack on the French fleet bottled up in the Aix Roads, 12 April 1809. His irregular methods terrified the French, but Admiral Gambier refused to support him, and the resulting court martial severely damaged Cochrane's career.*

battleships, 25 frigates and 200 other naval vessels. Despite capturing Flushing, and pushing up the River Scheldt, the army made slow progress, largely because of poor co-ordination between the naval and military leaders which left the army exposed on the malarial island of Walcheren, to struggle home ravaged by disease and with little to show for the effort. By this stage a more effective theatre for the deployment of British military resources had been opened.

Napoleon's overthrow of the Spanish monarchy in 1807 had sparked a nationalist uprising. This enabled a small British army, in combination with Portuguese and Spanish regulars, and the Spanish guerrillas, to pin down three French armies, opening Napoleon's 'Spanish Ulcer'. The British had finally found a European theatre in which maritime logistics outperformed land-based supply. It also increased the threat posed by maritime forces operating along the coast. Although the British army was far smaller than the French, seapower increased its effectiveness, while the French were paralysed by guerrilla activity, the Spanish regular forces and the sheer size of the country. Small British armies inserted in northern Europe between 1794 and 1809 had been speedily forced to evacuate. By contrast the Peninsula provided a succession of morale-boosting victories at a time when the French fleet was hard to find, and the other European powers were unable to fight. When Napoleon invaded Russia Wellington drove the French out of Spain, relying on the Royal Navy to shift his logistics base from Lisbon to Santander, and then across the Bay of Biscay into France.

Further afield, the British used their complete command of the sea to capture the last French naval bases in the West Indies and Indian Ocean: Martinique, Guadeloupe and Mauritius. They were followed by much of the Dutch East Indies. These acquisitions stopped privateer and cruiser operations in distant waters. The economic war began to turn in Britain's favour when Russia abandoned the Continental system in 1811. From that point Britain had little trouble raising the cash needed to bankroll her allies, while providing them with weapons, boots, uniforms and munitions. The addition of a sizeable army (over 100,000 men, not including hired forces) to the naval and economic dominance of the allied effort made Britain essential to the final defeat of Napoleon. As the only power consistently to oppose French hegemony, Britain used her insular position to provide an alternative vision of the political future for Spain, Russia and Germany. It was a role Britain and her seapower would have to play again.

Among Nelson's professional followers Captain Sir William Hoste, another Norfolk clergyman's son, operated with great effect in the Adriatic. At the battle of Lissa, 13 March 1811, he led four British frigates into action flying the signal 'Remember Nelson', and shattered a Franco-Italian frigate squadron nearly twice his own strength. After the war Sir William Parker, who was both St Vincent's nephew and Nelson's protégé, continued the personal link into the 1850s when, as commander-in-chief at Plymouth, he would enter John Fisher, the next British admiral of genius, into the service.

It was fitting that when Napoleon finally surrendered, on 15 July 1815, it was on board the battleship HMS *Bellerophon*, a veteran of the Glorious First of June, Cornwallis's Retreat, the Nile and Trafalgar. He was conveyed to St Helena aboard another 74-gunner, HMS *Northumberland*, under the command of Admiral Sir George Cockburn, a follower of Nelson and a leading practitioner of coastal warfare. The Royal Navy had set limits on Napoleon's empire, ground down his resources and made his ultimate success impossible. This was a significant enhancement of the role of seapower in continental affairs.

At the Congress of Vienna which ratified the peace, Britain retained the critical insular bases of Malta, Ceylon, Mauritius and Heligoland, together with the Cape. More importantly, France was removed from Belgium, which was united with the Netherlands, while Antwerp, Genoa and Venice were given to minor powers without serious naval ambitions. Within a generation, Britain had recovered from the loss of her American colonies, and used seapower to establish what amounted to a global maritime hegemony. Only one power now demonstrated the ability to challenge her.

CHAPTER NINE

The War of 1812

The man who burned the White House. Admiral Sir George Cockburn, with the public buildings of Washington blazing in the background. His facial expression suggests that he took a grim satisfaction in his handiwork. A protégé of Nelson, Cockburn was a master of amphibious operations and a skilled politician. He was chosen to take Napoleon to St Helena. (John Halls)

The War of 1812

DURING THE WAR OF Independence American warships and privateers had attacked British merchant shipping, resisted coastal operations, delayed the British use of Lake Champlain and carried the American cause into European waters. After the war the navy was disbanded, and was only reconstructed in 1793 to resist North African piracy. Before the new frigates were ready, Algiers was bought off with an annual indemnity. Consequently, the French were the first to feel the force of American power at sea. In 1797 they began seizing American ships, a move that rapidly escalated into the undeclared Caribbean 'Quasi-War' of 1798–1800. The Americans soon demonstrated their

THE THEATRE OF WAR, 1812–15

While the British held off American assaults on Canada they used amphibious operations to persuade the Americans to make peace. The operation against Washington in 1814 was a brilliant success, but the attempt at New Orleans in early 1815 was fatally compromised by inept military leadership.

British New Orleans campaign 22 November 1814 – 11 February 1815	
➡	British advance
➡	Jackson's night attack
⇢	British withdrawal
▥	fort
⌇	fortification

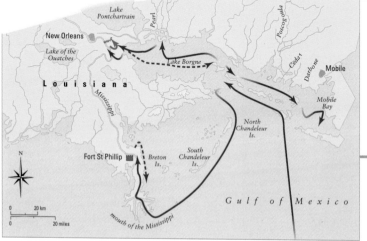

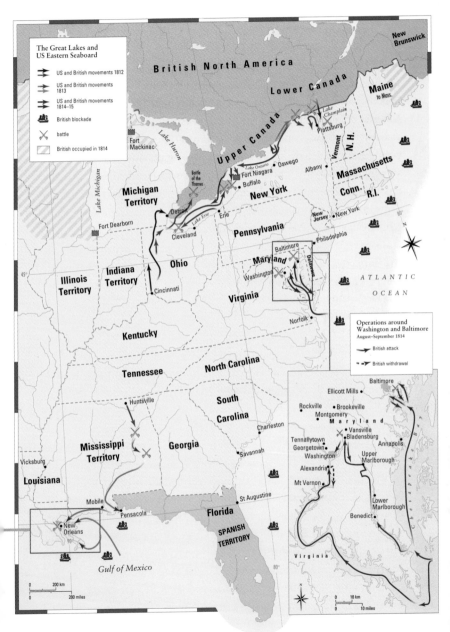

The Great Lakes and
US Eastern Seaboard

US and British movements 1812

US and British movements
1813

US and British movements
1814–15

British blockade

battle

British occupied in 1814

British North America

Lower Canada

Upper Canada

Maine
to Mass.

New
Brunswick

Fort
Mackinac

Lake Huron

Lake Michigan

Battle
of the
Thames

Detroit

Lake Ontario

Oswego

Fort Niagara

Buffalo

Albany

Vermont

N. H.

Massachusetts

Conn.

R.I.

Michigan
Territory

Fort Dearborn

Lake Erie

Erie

New York

New
Jersey

New York

Illinois
Territory

Indiana
Territory

Cincinnati

Cleveland

Ohio

Pennsylvania

Philadelphia

Baltimore

Maryland

Washington

Delaware

ATLANTIC

OCEAN

Virginia

Norfolk

Kentucky

Operations around
Washington and Baltimore
August–September 1814

British attack

British withdrawal

Tennessee

North Carolina

Huntsville

South
Carolina

Charleston

Savannah

Ellicott Mills

Baltimore

Rockville

Brookeville

Montgomery

Maryland

Tennallytown
Georgetown
Washington

Vansville
Bladensburg

Upper
Marlborough

Annapolis

Mississippi
Territory

Georgia

Vicksburg

Alexandria

Mt Vernon

Chesapeake Bay

Louisiana

Mobile

Pensacola

St Augustine

Florida

SPANISH
TERRITORY

Lower
Marlborough

Benedict

Virginia

New
Orleans

Gulf of Mexico

0   200 km

0   200 miles

0   10 km

0   10 miles

naval prowess, capturing a French frigate in February 1799. Later, the new navy blockaded Tripoli from 1803 to 1805.

In 1806 the Americans banned the import of British goods in retaliation for the harsh British interpretation of belligerent rights – the British searched neutral shipping and impressed American seamen. Whatever the legal rights of the issue, the British, who were fighting for survival, were not swayed by American protests, which they considered pro-French. America was now the largest neutral shipping nation, and so her goods and services were in great demand. Her shipping, a serious challenge to the British blockade and British prosperity, was deliberately targeted. Anglo-American tension exploded in June 1807, when HMS *Leopard* fired into the American frigate *Chesapeake*, forcing her to stop and surrender British deserters. In an attempt to isolate America from the European war, President Jefferson issued the Embargo Act which stopped Americans trading abroad, and had the effect of devastating the American economy. Napoleon then seized American ships in French ports. The Non-Intercourse Act of 1809 banned Americans from trading with Britain and France. In 1811 the USS *President* attacked the British sloop *Little Belt,* inflicting serious damage.

In June 1812 President Madison declared war. While he blamed British action at sea, his underlying motives were more complex. Madison's Republican Party was in crisis. By harnessing the energy of the expansionist lobby in the western states, who advocated the conquest of the Indian territory and Canada, he hoped to reunite his party and secure another term in office, relying on Napoleon's invasion of Russia to distract Britain. Although the British repealed the 'Orders in Council', the gesture was irrelevant. The American army launched a series of attacks on the Canadian frontier which ended in humiliation. The small force of British regulars and Canadian militia proved far more effective than Madison had imagined, while the American army was badly led and under-trained. On 16 August 1812 the American General William Hull surrendered 2,500 men to General Isaac Brock and his 1,300 Anglo-Canadian troops at Detroit. On the land frontier the Great

Lakes were the key to strategic mobility, and consequently powerful navies were created by both sides of Lake Erie and Lake Ontario.

At sea, the war began with an American frigate squadron cruising in the north Atlantic to protect home-bound merchant ships. The squadron was then broken up to cruise against British trade, but the American captains preferred the glory of capturing British warships. On 19 August General Hull's nephew Isaac Hull, commanding the USS *Constitution*, captured HMS *Guerriere* after a forty-minute action 700 miles east of Boston. The larger American ship mounted 24-pounder guns to the 18-pounders of the smaller, more lightly built British ship, and had a crew at least one quarter larger. Because the *Guerriere* was severely damaged, and a long way from home, she was burned. On 25 October the USS *United States*, commanded by Stephen Decatur, captured HMS *Macedonian* after a long gunnery duel in the mid-Atlantic, in which the same disparity of force applied. The prize was taken into the American Navy. Finally, on 29 November the *Constitution*, now commanded by William Bainbridge, took HMS *Java* off the coast of Brazil. Despite the usual disparity of force, the *Java* put up a good fight, and only surrendered after losing 122 killed and wounded, including her captain. Other single-ship actions in 1812 produced similar results. This was hardly surprising, as the British were fighting a world war with France and their best ships and men were in European waters.

At the end of 1812 the British blockaded the Chesapeake and Delaware bays, leaving New York and the New England states open to trade. This was done both to exploit Federalist opposition to the war, and to maintain the supply of grain to Wellington's army in Spain. Between March and June 1813 Admiral Sir George Cockburn launched an amphibious raiding campaign in Chesapeake Bay. In April the Americans raided York (modern Toronto) in Canada, burning the public buildings.

On 1 June 1813 HMS *Shannon* under Captain Philip Broke engaged the USS *Chesapeake*, commanded by Captain James Lawrence, off Boston in a frigate action of unequalled intensity. This was the finest single-ship action in the history of war at sea under sail. Both ships carried 18-pounder guns. Lawrence, a successful sloop commander, had just taken over the *Chesapeake*, which had a veteran crew of nearly 400 men. By contrast, Broke had commanded the *Shannon* for seven years, which he had devoted to the perfection of naval gunnery and the pursuit of honour. His crews were trained to hit the mark, fire rapidly and perform all drill in complete silence, so that orders could be clearly heard. Broke mounted 9-pounder guns on his quarterdeck, to shoot away the enemy ship's wheel. His whole career had been a preparation for single-ship action: during 1812 he had even refused to take mercantile prizes, so that he did not have to reduce his crew to man them.

After a long vigil off Boston, Broke was running short of food and, knowing the *Chesapeake* was ready to sail, sent in a 'challenge'. In the event Lawrence came out to meet him before it arrived. The American was confident in his own ability and the quality of his crew. The events of the day would demonstrate that his confidence was well placed, but he had underestimated his enemy. Once he saw the *Chesapeake* Broke moved out of sight of land and then took in sail while the American ship approached. He encouraged his crew by stressing their pre-eminence in gunnery, the need to have revenge for the earlier frigate actions, and the importance of firing into the hull to kill the crew, rather than trying to dismast the ship.

As the *Chesapeake* ran in from his after quarter, making over three knots to the *Shannon*'s two, Broke realized that Lawrence was approaching too quickly, and could not come up alongside. Against an ordinary foe this would not have mattered much, as little damage would have been done by the first broadside. However, *Shannon*'s guns fired as the *Chesapeake* came alongside, each aimed for the foremost gunport. They were loaded alternately with two balls, or one ball and grapeshot. Every British gun struck the Americans. The carronades on the upper deck were also double-loaded, and fired at the American forecastle battery, while the 9-pounder gun killed the American quartermaster. Lawrence, already wounded in the leg by a musket ball, realized he was going too fast, with his sails blanketing those of the *Shannon,* so he luffed up into the wind to lose speed. His gun crews were now able to fire, and they fired as fast as the British but, as they were to leeward and their weapons were not levelled, many rounds hit the *Shannon*'s waterline, rather than the gun crews. Only now, as the battle was fully joined, did Broke's insistence on silence begin to waver, the men punctuating their efforts with curses and cheers. Within minutes the well-laid British carronades had cleared the American upper deck, while only one third of the American crews were still working on the gun deck. The rest were dead or wounded. When the 9-pounder destroyed the *Chesapeake*'s wheel, her luff, instead of being arrested and the ship brought back on course, continued, assisted by her tattered rig, which picked up the wind and carried her off on a new course, exposing her stern to British fire. Finally *Chesapeake* lost way and drifted back towards the *Shannon.* With the American out of control, Broke wanted to manoeuvre his ship to continue the punishment at close range before boarding, but a chance shot cut his jib. Desperate to salvage a victory from this disaster, Lawrence ordered his men to prepare to board. As the men came up from the gun deck, Lawrence was hit in the groin by a second musket ball, and had to be helped down to the cockpit. *Chesapeake* was still drifting stern-first towards the *Shannon*, which was firing her main deck guns through the American's stern gallery, while the forecastle carronades and muskets swept her quarterdeck. Eventually, *Chesapeake* crashed stern-first into her opponent, about fifty feet aft of *Shannon*'s bow, and was held fast by the fluke of an anchor.

Although he had not planned to board himself Broke saw the chance and, as the only officer at hand, called for support and climbed aboard. Lawrence had only just reached the cockpit, where he famously called out: 'Tell the men to fire faster! Don't give up the ship!' The outnumbered Americans were driven back along the upper deck to the forecastle, where they broke and ran below. The ships then worked apart, leaving about sixty Englishmen on the *Chesapeake*'s upper deck. The fight was effectively over, the English held the upper deck, but three Americans, probably from one of the tops, attacked Broke. He killed the first with his sword, but the second clubbed him with a musket, knocking off his top hat, and the third slashed at him from the left side with a cutlass, cutting his skull open to the brains. His assailants were hacked to pieces by enraged British sailors. A small British ensign went up on the *Chesapeake* and *Shannon* ceased firing. When *Shannon*'s first lieutenant hauled down the ensign to hoist a larger flag, he and three other men were killed by a round of grapeshot from their own ship as

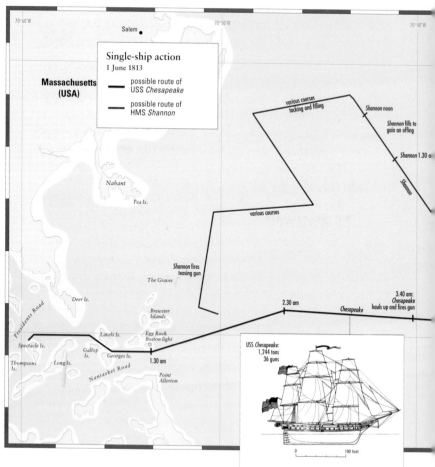

SHANNON–CHESAPEAKE ACTION

The finest single-ship action of all was fought between the USS Chesapeake and HMS Shannon, off Boston on 1 June 1813. These two almost perfectly matched ships met with only one thing in mind. Sir Philip Broke led James Lawrence out to sea, and then turned to wait. Lawrence had a well-manned ship ready for battle, and he was so anxious to fight that he came into action too fast. Against almost any other ship this would not have mattered, but Broke had dedicated his life to this supreme moment, preparing every detail for such a battle. The two ships were so close not a shot could miss the target, Shannon's crew fired first, and fired fast. Within eleven minutes it was all over. The painting shows the moment the Chesapeake went out of control, her wheel shot away and her rigging crippled. (John Christian Schetky)

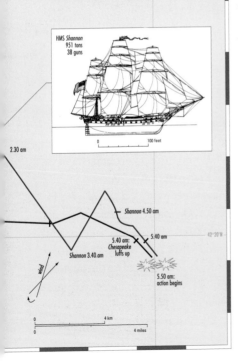

HMS *Shannon*
951 tons
38 guns

0   100 feet

42°30'N

2.30 am

Shannon 4.50 am

Shannon 3.40 am

5.40 am:
Chesapeake
luffs up

5.40 am

42°20'N

5.50 am:
action begins

Wind

0   4 km

0   4 miles

201

the gun captain presumed that anyone hauling down the British colours must be hostile. 'Friendly fire' is a very old problem. The remaining Americans were driven below, and the gratings secured over the hatches to keep them there. Lawrence, mortally wounded, called for the ship to be blown up, but no one responded. With the fight over Broke passed out, his terrible wound giving those around him little hope that he could survive.

The battle had taken only eleven minutes, timed by the *Shannon*'s gunner who was working in the powder room away from the carnage of the gun decks. In those eleven minutes, 148 Americans and 83 Englishmen had been killed or wounded, a higher toll than the *Victory* suffered at Trafalgar in six hours. The heavy casualties aboard the *Shannon* demonstrate just how good the American crew were, while their own losses, together with the annihilation of their officers, explain why the ship was taken. Lawrence died of peritonitis three days after the battle, just as his ship entered Halifax harbour. He became a national hero, and his cry 'Don't give up the ship!' became a motto for the United States Navy. After a near miraculous recovery, Broke came home in triumph and was made a baronet. He had earned his glory, restoring the good name of the Royal Navy after a run of poor form. Although he lived until 1840 and inspired the development of professional gunnery, Broke's wound denied him further sea service. Those who saw the shattered state of the *Chesapeake* needed no further encouragement to make gunnery the first requirement of the service.

This action provided a graphic illustration of the carnage inflicted by war at sea. The *Chesapeake*'s gun deck was strewn with shattered gun carriages and oak splinters, and splattered with blood, brains and mangled bodies, in fragments ranging from odd strips of flesh to severed limbs. The harsh reality of war ensured that in battle the dead were simply pitched overboard to clear the way. The wounded were sent to the cockpit below the waterline, where the surgeon and his assistant were ready with saws and scapels. There was no anaesthetic, apart from drink, and little hope of saving life if the wounds were internal.

Injured limbs where the bone had shattered, as was often the case with low velocity grapeshot and musket balls, were invariably amputated with more speed than skill. Nelson's arm was taken off so badly that he had to have the stump re-opened and the nerve secured. Broke was more fortunate: his injury was so severe that his surgeon could do nothing but dress the wound and pray. He was brought through by the same singleness of purpose and iron will that had kept him at sea for seven long years in search of glory.

Late in 1813 the struggle on Lake Erie took a decisive turn when Commodore Oliver Hazard Perry captured the British fleet at Put in Bay. His success was quickly followed up on land, at the battle of the Thames on 4 October, when the Americans smashed a tiny British and Native American army, killing their inspirational leader Tecumseh. On Lake Ontario the two fleets spent their time building ever larger ships and skirmishing, neither side being prepared to fight when their forces were inferior. This astonishing shipbuilding effort progressed rapidly from sloops to frigates, and culminated with the commissioning of HMS *St Lawrence*, a 100-gun three-decker. This ship gave the British undisputed command of the lake. At the end of the war she had sisters on the stocks at Kingston, while two American rivals were almost complete at Sackett's Harbour. Although these lake ships were smaller than their salt water cousins, needing no water and few stores for their short cruises, they were still colossal vessels to build in what was little more than a wilderness.

Later that autumn an American army advanced down the St Lawrence towards Montreal, but was heavily defeated by a small Canadian force at Chrysler's Farm on 17 November. The major American offensive for 1814, on the Niagara front, was halted at the battle of Lundy's Lane, on 25 July, although the American army redeemed its reputation after the abject failures of 1812. Their second-in-command, Winfield Scott, would be the architect of the post-war American army, and was the hero of the Mexican War of 1846–8.

The end of the war in Europe in April 1814 allowed the British government to devote greater resources to the American theatre, particularly troops from Wellington's army. The strategy was to rely on coastal raids, and a major offensive along the Lake Champlain route to force the Americans to pull back from Canada and make peace. Between May and December Cockburn resumed work in the Chesapeake Bay area, under a new commander-in-chief, Admiral Sir Alexander Cochrane. In August Cockburn landed General Sir Robert Ross and his army in the River Patuxent to march on Washington. On 24 August the British advance guard attacked a larger American force at Bladensburg, which ran away before Ross could reach the battlefield. That night Ross and Cockburn entered Washington, ate President Madison's celebration dinner and set fire to the public buildings in retaliation for York. When the scorched presidential mansion was whitewashed it acquired the nickname 'the White House'. The Americans had already burned Washington Navy Yard, destroying four warships.

In September the British attacked Baltimore. During the initial reconnaissance, Ross, this time too far ahead of his troops, was killed. Despite a naval bombardment of Fort McHenry on the 12th and 14th, the army was unable to penetrate the American defences and withdrew. The spectacle of rockets and bombs fired from the fleet, their fuses burning brightly as they arched through the night sky, inspired Francis Scott Key to pen *The Star Spangled Banner*, one of the more unlikely products of seapower. Before the Baltimore attack, however, the biggest British operation of the war had been brought to an ignominious end. General Prevost, the cautious governor-general of Canada and defender of the St Lawrence frontier, was ordered to advance south with 11,000 regulars. Instead of attacking the weak American defences at Plattsburg, New York, on the western shore of Lake Champlain, he ordered his naval force to attack the American ships lying on the flank of the defences. On 11 September the British squadron was decisively defeated by Commodore Thomas Macdonough's American force. Prevost, who had no enthusiasm for the offensive, retreated into Canada. Recalled in disgrace, his failure persuaded the British to accept the status quo.

'And the rocket's red glare, the bombs bursting in air.' The British flotilla attacking Fort McHenry at Baltimore with mortars and rockets, 13 September 1814. Francis Scott Key, then on board a British ship, penned the lines that became the American national anthem after watching the attack.

Before news of the Anglo-American peace signed at Ghent on Christmas Eve 1814 could reach the war zone, the British attacked New Orleans. This time their general, Wellington's brother-in-law Sir Edward Pakenham, was as rash as Prevost had been cautious. Rather than wait to secure control of the Mississippi River, or turn the flank of Andrew Jackson's strong position on the east bank of the river, Pakenham led a frontal assault on 8 January 1815. The attack failed and Pakenham was killed, one of 2,036 British casualties.

At sea, the last major action of the war occurred on 15 January 1815, when the USS *President* under Captain Stephen Decatur put to sea from New York. She was pursued and captured by a British frigate squadron. As the largest American prize of the war, one of the three 'super-frigates', *President* was taken to Britain, carefully measured and a replica built in order to retain her name on the list of the Royal Navy. The first deployment of the new HMS *President* was to the American station in the early 1830s, flying the flag of Sir George Cockburn, the man who burnt Washington in 1814. It hardly needs to be observed that this was a period of Anglo-American tension.

During the war American privateers captured numerous British merchant ships, but few prizes got back to America; meanwhile, the

American merchant marine was driven from the seas. When the British blockade was finally applied to New England in 1814, several states considered leaving the Union. Once the British and Canadians demonstrated that they would resist the invasion, this was a war America could not win. Only the sterling performance of her small navy, and the improvement in the American army, enabled Madison to escape the disaster he had brought upon his country.

The early success of the American Navy proved crucial to the long-term existence of the service. The pursuit of 'honour' by the naval officer corps had gone down well with a nation starved of glory. After the war the service was given a major boost, rather than being demobilized, although attempts to turn it into a battlefleet sea control navy were premature. After 1812 the British took America seriously as a naval power, an honour they accorded very few nations.

The value of a name. Having captured an American super-frigate the British took care to copy her design, and when she proved uneconomic to repair, built a replica to carry the name as HMS President. In this way navies have always celebrated success, and built on the legacy of victory.

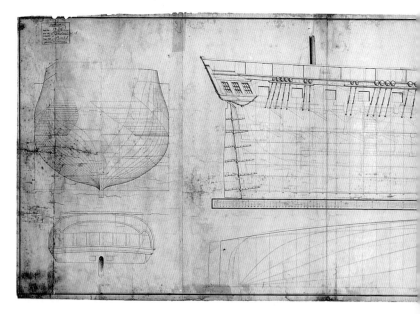

The capture of the USS President, *15 January 1815, by a squadron of British frigates.*
HMS Endymion *had hung on to the American ship and crippled her rigging, forcing*
Captain Stephen Decatur to stand and fight. After a short engagement with
Endymion *he surrendered as other British ships came up.*

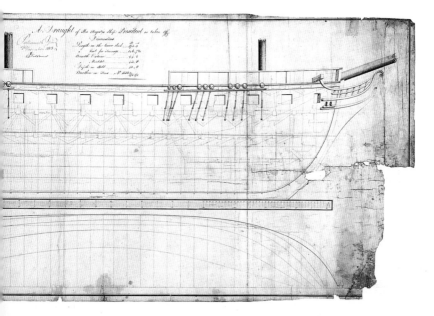

CHAPTER TEN

Pax Britannica? The Last Years of Seapower Under Sail 1815–50

A Chinese war junk exploding under fire from the East India Company British iron steam warship HEIC Nemesis in Anson's Bay, near Canton, 8 January 1841. Steamers with shell-firing guns enabled the British to take their power close inshore, opening rivers and harbours to the full weight of naval firepower. In this war the object was to increase trade. (E. Duncan)

Pax Britannica? The Last Years of Seapower Under Sail 1815–50

IN MANY WAYS 1815 marked the end of the contest for seapower in the age of sailing navies. Although Holland, France, Spain and even Russia had competed, Britain was now the undisputed ruler of the waves. Britain retained her dominance to the end of the sailing ship era, although the nature of war at sea was changing, and the introduction of shell-firing guns and steam engines presaged the arrival of a new order after 1850.

Britain used her dominance of the sea, financial power and primacy in the industrial revolution both to support an aggressive commercial policy, and to maintain an equilibrium of power in Europe in an attempt to avoid costly and unproductive wars. The Royal Navy was reconstructed as a long-term deterrent. Between 1815 and 1830 a new battle fleet was built, using the finest timber, scientific methods of wood preservation, and an improved structural system. This new battle fleet proved so successful that it became obsolete long before it became unserviceable.

While the British battle fleet was maintained at 250,000 tons, the French fleet was halved from 180,000 tons in 1815 to 84,000 in 1840. France had accepted her naval role, well behind the British but far ahead of any other power. Consequently her strategy and procurement had a somewhat schizophrenic appearance, emphasizing frigates designed for commerce destruction and battleships intended to break a British blockade, or act as a sea control force against lesser states. While the combined Russian battle fleets in the Baltic and Black seas were consistently larger than the French, reaching nearly 160,000 tons in 1840, they were badly built of inferior timber, and usually a generation behind the latest western designs. In the 1830s the Russian fleets caused some alarm in Britain, but France remained Britain's only significant rival at sea. The Americans built a few heavily armed battleships to break a British blockade and release smaller ships to wage a *guerre de course*.

Simply because her security depended on the sea, Britain had no desire to share naval power with other states, and began to act as the 'policeman' of the oceans within weeks of Waterloo. When the Americans and the Russians began to talk about suppressing North African piracy, Admiral Lord Exmouth took a fleet to demand that Algiers end piracy and the enslavement of Christians. The following day Exmouth attacked. Supported by Dutch ships, he manoeuvred in close, knocked down the harbour defences, burnt the fleet and bombarded the city. Although British casualties were high (16 per cent were killed or wounded), the Algerians capitulated.

The use of British naval power in Europe was restricted by the close Franco-Russian alignment between 1815 and 1830, which led to the declaration of the British 'Two Power Standard' in 1817 and stated that the Royal Navy should be equal to the combined strength of the next two naval powers. This 'standard' remained at the heart of British naval policy for a century. In 1823 the Franco-Russian alliance re-established the absolutist regime in Spain, despite British opposition. But the British prevented Spain and her allies from recovering Spain's American empire, which had been largely liberated by Lord Cochrane's mercenary fleets. As Foreign Secretary, George Canning made it clear that the British fleet provided the power behind the American Monroe Doctrine which opposed European conquests in the Americas. Only the Royal Navy could stop France or Russia from operating in the New World.

The last great naval battle of the sailing ship era arose out of the Greek War of Independence, 1822–32. In an attempt to control the conflict Britain joined France and Russia, which had wider ambitions. When Sir Edward Codrington led the combined fleets into Navarino Bay on 20 October 1827 determined to forestall a Turkish attack on the Greek island of Hydra, battle was inevitable. The numerous but smaller ships of the Turco-Egyptian fleet were almost annihilated in a savage close-range battle by the superior firepower of the allied ships, especially Codrington's flagship the new 84-gun *Asia*. While a new ministry in London considered Navarino 'untoward' and sacked Codrington, the French and Russians celebrated a rare victory.

The French followed up Navarino by invading Algeria in 1830. Admiral Duperre's fleet, 100 warships and 350 transports, landed 38,000 troops near Algiers, beginning a war that would last another twenty years. Britain only permitted the French operation because the French promised they would leave once they had chastised the Algerines. However, the Algerian expedition failed in its primary objective, and the unpopular king, Charles X, was overthrown, breaking the Franco-Russian alignment. Britain could now play off her rivals in Europe while expanding her global economic interests. This gave the chief architect of British external policy between 1830 and 1850, Lord Palmerston, the freedom to use naval power in Europe. He supervised the creation of an independent Belgium by deploying a fleet

Admiral Baudin's French fleet bombarding and taking Fort St Juan d'Ulloa at Vera Cruz in Mexico, 27 November 1838. This engagement was notable for the successful use of explosive shells from ships towed into place by steamers, demonstrating the new-found offensive power of fleets against old fortifications. (Jean Gudin)

A French battleship in the last days of sail, showing the full cross section of uses to which every on-board space was put.

in the Channel both to force Holland to relinquish her claims and to keep the French out of the area. In July 1833 Palmerston's policy was advanced by Captain Charles Napier, serving as a mercenary in the Portuguese civil war, who secured the triumph of the pro-British regime off Cape St Vincent.

During the 1830s shell-firing guns, developed by the French artillerist General Henri Paixhans, were introduced into service by the major navies. Although the shells were inaccurate and often unreliable, they had the potential to destroy a wooden warship in as many minutes as conventional cannon required hours. The first use of the new weapons suggested that they could change the strategic balance between the land and the sea. A French squadron under Admiral Baudin resolved a financial dispute with Mexico by bombarding and capturing the fortress of St Juan D'Ulloa at Vera Cruz on 27 November 1838, and their success was largely attributed to the shell guns.

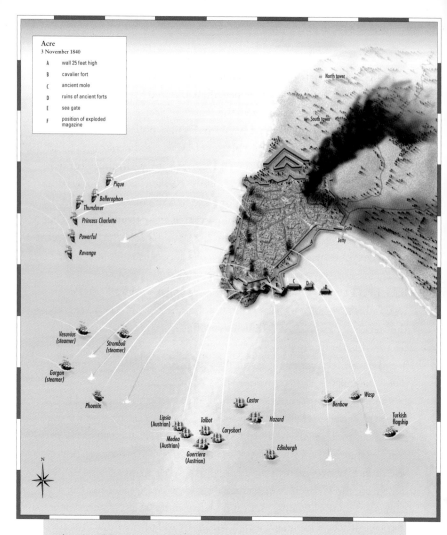

Acre
3 November 1840

A   wall 25 feet high

B   cavalier fort

C   ancient mole

D   ruins of ancient forts

E   sea gate

F   position of exploded magazine

North tower

South tower

Gate

Jetty

Pique

Bellerophon

Thunderer

Princess Charlotte

Powerful

Revenge

Vesuvius (steamer)

Stromboli (steamer)

Gorgon (steamer)

Phoenix

Lipsia (Austrian)

Medea (Austrian)

Guerriera (Austrian)

Talbot

Caryshort

Castor

Hazard

Edinburgh

Benbow

Wasp

Turkish flagship

N

ACRE, 3 NOVEMBER 1840

The campaign culminated in a full-scale attack on the fortress at Acre, the last Egyptian strong point, on 3 November 1840. The object was to open a breach in the southern sea defences, through which the Turkish troops were to storm the city. In the event a shell from the fleet detonated a large magazine, causing such devastation that the Egyptians evacuated the fortress that night.

In 1839–40 the fate of the Ottoman Empire hung in the balance. The rebellious pasha of Egypt, Mehemet Ali, had seized Syria and Palestine, built a powerful fleet, acquired the Turkish fleet by treachery, and annihilated the Ottoman army. With French political support he seemed set to overthrow the sultan. However, Palmerston secured the support of Russia, Prussia and Austria to guarantee Turkish independence, and directed Commodore Napier, who conducted a brilliant amphibious campaign along the Syrian coast. Command of the sea enabled Napier to cut off the Egyptian army from its base. The British fleet then attacked Acre, their last stronghold, on 3 November 1840. During a heavy and accurate bombardment, the main Egyptian magazine exploded. The Egyptians abandoned the town and retreated back into Egypt. Within the month Napier had forced Mehemet Ali to restore his allegiance to the Ottoman sultan, in the process destroying the French position in the Middle East. Although the French had a large fleet in the Mediterranean they were deterred from intervening by the speed of Napier's campaign, and the mobilization of British reserves. They recognized that they would lose a maritime war.

Palmerston also waged war on China between 1839 and 1843. To secure trade and access to Far Eastern markets he relied on the dynamic use of amphibious power. Admiral Sir William Parker used Indian Navy steamships to tow British battleships into the Chinese rivers, where they knocked down major forts and landed British troops who cut the Grand Canal that supplied Beijing with rice. The combination of naval firepower and the tactical mobility of steam had cracked open the shell of the Celestial Empire. Steam had expanded the strategic power of the sea: the only limit to the range and projection of British power was the presence of navigable water.

Although steam had been used at sea from the 1820s, paddlewheel ships were never front-line warships. The paddlewheels and machinery were terribly exposed, while they lacked the firepower of sailing ships and could not sail well enough to maintain station in a sailing fleet without burning coal. By the 1840s steam had added a new dimension to the strategic and tactical mobility of maritime power, and were especially good instruments for amphibious power projection. By 1845 a new propeller, the screw, had been adopted, replacing the bulky, vulnerable wheel with a compact submerged drive. The screw also enabled steam and sail to be combined in a single ship.

Between 1846 and 1848 the United States used naval power to defeat Mexico and seize huge areas of territory. Landing at Vera Cruz in 1847, General Winfield Scott's army of less than 10,000 men captured Mexico City within six months. American naval forces also occupied California and blockaded the Mexican coast. The United States secured Texas, California and other areas totalling 500,000 square miles, for which they paid Mexico $15,000,000. Naval power was critical to the American success.

In the late 1840s rising political tension in Europe prompted the British to increase the size of their active fleets. Palmerston employed his favourite commanders, Parker and Napier, in the Mediterranean and the English Channel. This mobilization supported British interests during the

European revolutions of 1848, and deterred any ambitions the new French Second Republic might have harboured to export its political difficulties. The power and flexibility of these fleets, which operated year round, in all weathers, was reflected in the prestige and influence of the British state.

Only in 1850 did the sailing battleship, the ultimate instrument of seapower since the sixteenth century, give way to a new dominant instrument, her half-sister the screw steam battleship. This compromise between the old order and the new survived a bare decade before further changes created new and more terrible instruments of naval power, although it is fitting that the precursor of the big gun battleship was the latest incarnation of the *Royal Sovereign*. After being laid down as a wooden sailing battleship in the 1840s this ship had been converted into a screw steam battleship, and then cut down, fitted with armour and four rotating turrets. With her masts and yards long gone, and her firepower now reduced from 120 guns to five, this strange hybrid carried on where her ancestors had left off, providing the visible symbol of British naval deterrence.

The last British sailing battleship, HMS Royal Sovereign *(IV) was converted initially into a steam ship, and was then cut down, armoured and fitted with revolving turrets by 1864. In this form she was a direct threat to any naval base in Europe, and served to deter war, much as the* Sovereign of the Seas *had back in the 1630s. The purpose of seapower remained to deter, and only if necessary to fight.*

Battlefleet tonnages of the major powers 1650–1850

The figures represent effective useable tonnage (in thousands of tons)

	Britain	France	Holland	Spain	Denmark	Sweden	Russia (Baltic)	Russia (Black Sea)	USA
1650	49	21	29		25	28			
1655	90	18	64		21	28			
1660	88	20	62		16	23			
1665	102	36	81		26	31			
1670	84	114	102		32	34			
1675	95	138	89		29	35			
1680	132	135	66		33	18			
1685	128	123	76		34	31			
1690	113	122	58		31	35			
1695	152	190	84		33	40			
1700	174	176	97		42	48			
1705	170	167	94		50	55			
1710	171	158	101		55	50	3		
1715	168	102	84	9	51	37	27		
1720	146	45	68	13	48	34	42		
1725	153	78	52	25	41	31	49		
1730	162	68	47	67	42	27	55		
1735	165	76	53	81	48	35	53		
1740	170	85	45	84	48	33	30		
1745	174	80	44	51	55	35	44		
1750	205	97	46	35	58	38	53		

	Britain	France	Holland	Spain	Denmark	Sweden	Russia (Baltic)	Russia (Black Sea)	USA
1755	210	133	39	93	56	37	45		
1760	265	128	39	115	58	40	48		
1765	291	146	43	103	62	42	39		
1770	276	174	45	139	64	37	47		
1775	260	152	38	161	69	40	62		
1780	255	194	39	148	71	40	56		
1785	305	183	84	155	69	48	88	5	
1790	334	231	87	188	71	31	114	14	
1795	312	180	51	203	70	26	114	24	
1800	330	136	35	176	67	29	114	31	
1805	360	129	33	104	49	25	123	32	
1810	413	148	31	77	4	27	85	30	
1815	358	179	52	47	4	27	92	47	11
1820	330	172	20	36	7	26	80	50	28
1825	288	157	18	13	7	18	94	50	28
1830	256	124	15	8	10	18	98	54	28
1835	260	105	16	8	15	19	90	48	28
1840	257	84	16	5	16	19	107	56	29
1845	246	84	13	3	16	19	105	52	26
1850	249	103	16	3	13	19	106	60	30

Taken from J. Glete, *Navies and Nations: Warships, Navies and State Building in Europe and America, 1500–1850*, Stockholm 1993.

Biographies

ANSON, GEORGE, LATER LORD ANSON (1697–1762)
Sent to attack the Spanish empire in the Pacific in 1740, Anson's iron
will survived the loss of all but one of his ships and most of his men to
capture a treasure galleon and return home in 1744 with fabulous wealth.
Thereafter, he ran the navy until his death. A master of tactics, training,
leadership, strategy and politics, he was the greatest sea officer of the
eighteenth century.

BART, JEAN (1650–1702)
Born in the Spanish Netherlands, Bart achieved mythic status as a corsair
and privateer in the war of the League of Augsburg, attacking English and
Dutch shipping. Subsequent biographies have undervalued his particular
genius for the *guerre de course*.

BLAKE, ROBERT (1599–1657)
After distinguished service in the English Civil War, Blake was sent to
instil order, discipline and loyalty into the Commonwealth navy in 1649.
He commanded many battles in the First Anglo-Dutch War, 1652–4, and
was largely responsible for the linear tactics and the emphasis on firepower,
that defeated the Dutch. In 1657 he annihilated a Spanish treasure fleet at
Santa Cruz.

COCHRANE, THOMAS, LATER THE EARL OF DUNDONALD (1775–1860)
The model for most naval fictional heroes, Cochrane captured a Spanish
warship by subterfuge and daring in 1800, and later commanded frigates
off the coast of Spain with tremendous success, crippling French coastal
shipping. A radical MP from 1806, he had enemies in high places, notably
Earl St Vincent. In 1809 he led a fireship and explosion vessel attack at Aix
Roads which left the French fleet in disarray, but Admiral Lord Gambier
baulked at the opportunity this provided. In 1812 he devised a gas warfare
plan that was rejected as inhuman but not impractical. He was imprisoned
for a stock market fraud in 1814 and expelled from the navy. In 1817 he
commanded the Peruvian and Chilean fleets to gain independence from

Spain, and did the same for Brazil against Portugal, but was less successful in Greece. Reinstated in the Royal Navy in 1832 for the deterrent value of his reputation, he had skill, daring, resolve, invention and courage, both moral and physical; but his avarice and lack of political acumen held him back.

COCKBURN, SIR GEORGE (1772–1853)
Cockburn served St Vincent and Nelson, and was sent on missions of great sensitivity. He excelled in coastal warfare, epitomized by the capture of Washington in 1814. He carried Napoleon into exile on St Helena in 1815, and Cochrane's post-war service was largely ashore.

COLBERT, JEAN BAPTISTE (1619–83)
As Minister of the Marine from 1669, Colbert revived the French Navy in a mercantilist programme to secure the empire of the seas for Louis XIV. He built the ships, dockyards, administration and schools, recruited officers and provided funds. After his death his son, the Marquis de Seignelay, continued his work until 1690, but Louis XIV preferred military conquest, and downgraded the fleet after Barfleur. Colbert's great achievements were only exceeded by the complete French naval failure after his death.

DECATUR, STEPHEN (1779–1820)
Decatur rose to fame through his daring destruction of a captured American frigate in Tripoli harbour in 1804. In 1812 he commanded the USS *United States* and captured HMS *Macedonian* in the mid Atlantic. Blockaded for most of the war, he finally escaped from New York in the USS *President*, but surrendered to a British squadron after a running action. Escaping censure he went to the Mediterranean, and brought Algiers to terms. He was killed by Commodore James Barron in a duel over the *Chesapeake–Leopard* affair of 1807. Had he lived, he was a serious contender for the US presidency.

DE GRASSE, FRANÇOIS-JOSEPH PAUL (1722–88)
De Grasse entered the navy in 1738 and secured his first command in the West Indies in 1781. In September 1781, he prevented the badly handled British fleet off the Chesapeake Capes from relieving Cornwallis's army at Yorktown, ending the last British effort to subdue America. The following

spring he fared less well, being outmanoeuvred at St Kitts and, on 12 April 1782, he was defeated and captured at the Saintes. De Grasse was a good officer, but not equal to his British contemporaries, Hood, Rodney and Howe.

DE RUYTER, MICHIEL ADRIANSZOON (1607–76)

Raised at sea, de Ruyter inherited the mantle of Tromp and reformed the Dutch fleet to meet the new order of fleet tactics reliant on gunnery. He won the Four Days battle, and crowned the Second Anglo-Dutch War with his brilliant raid on Chatham in 1667, humiliating the English with a demonstration of skill and enterprise. In the Third War he held off the Anglo-French fleet, despite a marked inferiority in firepower and numbers, a masterpiece of the strategic defensive. He died of his wounds after defeating a larger French fleet off Sicily. A master seaman, tactician and strategist, he was the greatest sea officer of the seventeenth century.

DUGUAY-TROUIN, RENÉ (1673–1736)

Duguay secured his first privateer command in 1691, and went on to enter the French Navy as a captain, taking whole convoys and finally capturing Rio de Janeiro in 1711.

HOOD, SAMUEL, VISCOUNT (1724–1816)

After a solid career Hood appeared to have been passed over, until the American War of Independence provided him with a chance to command. He proved outstanding. In 1782 he comprehensively outmanoeuvred de Grasse at St Kitts and played a major part at the Saintes in April. However, he was outspokenly, and rightly, critical of Rodney's failure to follow up the battle. He inspired younger officers (notably Nelson) to believe that more initiative should be given to subordinates, and more risks run to annihilate the enemy. In 1793–4 he commanded in the Mediterranean against the French, occupying Toulon, and capturing Corsica, but was dismissed for criticizing the Admiralty. Nelson considered Hood 'the first man in the Navy'. There can be no higher praise.

Howe, Richard, Earl (1726–99)

A captain at 20, Hood led the fleet at Quiberon Bay in 1759. Promoted admiral in 1770, he commanded in America from 1776, and sought a political settlement to the rebellion. He demonstrated transcendent tactical skill against a superior French fleet, but resigned after a disagreement with the government in 1778. He devoted his time ashore to reforming tactics and signalling, laying the foundations of the tight control he preferred. In 1782 he led a brilliant relief of Gibraltar, and in 1794 won the battle of the Glorious First of June, reasserting British mastery of the Atlantic. In 1797 Howe came out of retirement to settle the Spithead Mutiny. Popularly known as 'Black Dick' from his swarthy complexion, Howe was a model of integrity and revered throughout the navy.

Jervis, John, later Earl St Vincent (1735–1823)

Jervis led Saunders's fleet carrying Wolfe's army to Quebec in 1759. After commanding the successful West Indian campaigns of 1794, he went to the Mediterranean and defeated the Spanish fleet off Cape St Vincent with the help of Nelson who anticipated Jervis's intentions. Created Earl St Vincent, he later commanded in the Channel, but his period as First Sea Lord, in which he attempted to reform naval administration, made him many enemies. A shrewd judge of character and talent, in 1803 he appointed Nelson to the Mediterranean, and Cornwallis to the Channel fleet, putting in place the men who defeated Napoleon's strategy. Jervis carefully manufactured the public image of the harsh, inflexible commander, but in private he was warm and companionable, enjoying practical jokes. St Vincent took on the mantle of the father of the service, and carried it with great dignity and utter dedication.

Jones, John Paul (1747–92)

A Scots-born American naval officer, Jones won the first naval victories of the new nation. After merchant service, Jones was commissioned lieutenant in the Continental Navy. In 1777 he took the *Ranger* to France, to attack British shipping and harbours. After capturing HMS *Drake* Jones shifted to the *Bonhomme Richard*, and took HMS *Serapis* in 1779 in a severe action, where his willpower alone secured the victory over a more powerful and better manned enemy. He joined the Russian fleet, and despite all his celebrity, his subsequent career was disappointing.

NAPIER, SIR CHARLES (1786–1860)

Promoted captain for an act of 'uncommon bravery', Napier served in the Mediterranean from 1810 to 1814, capturing ships, islands and convoys. In 1814 he commanded the rocket boats that fired on Baltimore. Later, he pioneered the use of iron steamships, served Portugal as a mercenary, won the Syrian campaign of 1840, served in Parliament and commanded the Baltic fleet in 1854, but was dismissed as a scapegoat for his political masters.

NELSON, HORATIO, LATER LORD NELSON (1758–1805)

A captain at 20, Nelson attracted the notice of Lord Hood who took him to the Mediterranean in 1793, where he demonstrated transcendent qualities of initiative, insight and daring. When Jervis took command, Nelson retained his trust with his brilliant anticipation of his intentions at St Vincent. Despite losing his arm at Tenerife in 1797, Nelson hunted down the French expedition, which he finally located in Egypt, and annihilated at the battle of Nile, which was distinguished by the broad permissive instructions Nelson issued to his captains. Sent to the Baltic in 1801, he won the battle of Copenhagen by sheer hard fighting and force of character. In 1803 he was appointed to the Mediterranean, and in 1805 pursued the French fleet from Toulon to the West Indies, and returned to blockade it in Cádiz, with the Spanish. When the allies emerged Nelson used a dynamic tactical approach. All his captains were given the widest latitude as to how they might best distinguish themselves, in order to break up and annihilate the allied formation in close-range action. Nelson died in battle, as he had long anticipated. Although equally famous today for his relationship with Emma Hamilton, Nelson was first and foremost a genius of naval warfare, and Britain's first truly national hero.

PEPYS, SAMUEL (1633–1703)

Pepys was appointed to the Navy Board, administering the fleet in peace and war. In 1673 he became Secretary to the Board of Admiralty, reforming the service. He was finally forced to retire after the Revolution of 1688, being too closely linked to James II (who was Lord High Admiral from 1660 and king from 1685–8). The posthumous publication of his diary made him famous.

RODNEY, GEORGE BRYDGES, LATER LORD RODNEY (1719–92)
Rodney served with distinction between 1739 and 1763, latterly commanding expeditions in the West Indies. His political and social ambitions invariably outran his prize fortune, and he was often accused of neglecting his duty, or at least subordinating it to motives of profit. In 1780 he routed a Spanish fleet while relieving Gibraltar in the 'Moonlight battle' notable for its daring tactics and continued action after dark. In the West Indies he stabilized the strategic situation, before devoting his efforts to exploiting the immense prize of the Dutch island of St Eustasius. Unfortunately, much of his loot was captured by the French. On 12 April 1782 he routed the French fleet under de Grasse off the Saintes passage, exploiting a shift in the wind.

ROOKE, SIR GEORGE (1650–1709)
Rooke received his admiral's flag in 1690, fighting at Beachy Head. He destroyed the stranded French ships at La Hougue in 1692, and in 1693 escorted the Smyrna convoy, struggling against overwhelming odds. Rooke was rigid and slow-moving, failing to attack Cádiz in 1702 and only saving his career with the attack on Vigo. A rigid exponent of linear tactics, he captured Gibraltar in 1704, and defeated the French fleet at Malaga.

SUFFREN, PIERRE ANDRÉ (1729–88)
Suffren initially served the Knights of Malta, before entering the French Navy, only to be captured by the British in 1747 and 1759. Sent to the East Indies in 1781, he fought out a series of severe actions with Admiral Hughes, in which the superior tactical skill, aggression and insight of Suffren was negated by the poor performance of his captains. His reputation remains high, more because of the failure of other French admirals than because of any outstanding merit he may have had.

SURCOUF, ROBERT (1773–1827)
A French slaver who became a brilliant privateer in the Indian Ocean between 1795 and 1809, Surcouf captured many large merchant ships. His skill enabled him to operate despite British dominance of the sea. He refused Napoleon's offer of a naval captaincy, and returned home to organize more privateers.

TOURVILLE, ANNE HILARION DE COTENTIN, COMTE DE (1642–1701)
Having served the Knights of Malta Tourville joined the French Navy in 1672. A fine seaman and analyst of naval tactics, he commanded the French fleet 1689–93. In 1690 the limitations of contemporary logistics and his caution denied France the full fruits of the triumph at Beachy Head. In 1692 he was ordered into battle with inferior forces, and after holding off Russell's fleet for a day, many of his ships were destroyed at La Hougue. He captured the Smyrna convoy in 1693, a masterpiece of commerce warfare, and is remembered as the greatest of French admirals.

TROMP, MAERTEN HARPERTSZOON (1597–1653)
A born seaman, Tromp annihilated the Spanish at the Downs in 1639, the last major action of the mêlée era. In 1652 he escorted Dutch shipping through the Channel against more powerful English forces. Although his leadership and skill secured some Dutch successes, ultimately superior English firepower and linear tactics proved too much. Adored by his men and respected by the English, Tromp was killed in battle.

VILLENEUVE, PIERRE CHARLES (1763–1806)
Villeneuve gained rapid promotion after the Revolution, despite his limited abilities. He commanded the rear at the Nile in 1798, and escaped Nelson's assault. While Napoleon considered him 'lucky', and appointed him to command at Toulon in 1804, Villeneuve was morbidly aware of the vast gulf that lay between his fleet and the British, and between himself and Nelson. In 1805 he sailed to the West Indies, fled from Nelson and was beaten by Calder on his return. He lacked the moral courage to head for Brest, running instead to Cádiz. Ordered to support an invasion of Sicily, Villeneuve and his allied fleet was annihilated by Nelson, the result he had anticipated. Released in 1806, he either committed suicide or was murdered.

Further reading

The starting point for any serious study of this subject is to stress the importance of taking a wider view of war at sea than has usually been the case. The role of the state in the development of navies, and of navies in the development of states is analysed in *Navies and Nations: Warships, Navies and State Building in Europe and America, 1500–1850,* Jan Glete (Stockholm 1993), a work of astonishing scope and erudition. A different and equally compelling approach is adopted in *Seapower and Naval Warfare, 1650–1830,* Richard Harding (London 1998), which examines the strategic exploitation of the sea. *The Rise and Fall of British Naval Mastery* (London 1976) by Paul Kennedy provides an important overview of the most significant naval power of the past 500 years, and of its interaction with the domestic and international economies and with other nations. The old standard, A. T. Mahan's *Influence of Sea Power* series covering the period between 1660 and 1815 (Boston 1890–1905), is still useful for the insight it offers into the late nineteenth century navalist mind, and the development of strategic ideas. However, they must be used with care, and were never intended to be scholarly histories.

The development of all types of warship is examined in *The Ship of the Line,* Brian Lavery (London 1983), *The Line of Battle: the sailing warship 1650–1840* ed. Lavery (London 1992) and *The Seventy-Four Gun Ship,* J. Boudriot (Rotherfield 1986). Naval social life is best approached through *The Wooden World: An Anatomy of the Georgian Navy,* N. A. M. Rodger (London 1986), naval organization through *British Naval Administration in the Age of Walpole,* D. A. Baugh (Princeton 1965) and *Yellow Jack and the Worm: British Naval Administration in the West Indies, 1739–1748,* D. G. Crewe (Liverpool 1993).

The Royal Dockyards, 1690–1815: architecture and engineering works of the sailing navy, J. Coad (Aldershot 1989) and *The Royal Dockyards during the Revolutionary and Napoleonic Wars,* R. Morriss (Leicester 1983) provide invaluable insight into the link between infrastructure and naval power. John Brewer's *The Sinews of Power: War, Money and the English State 1690–1763*

(London 1989) provides an overview of how one state developed the systems to fund a world-class navy. *Corsairs and Navies*, J. R. Bromley (London 1987) examines other forms of seapower, a theme developed in *British Privateering Enterprise*, D. Starkey (Exeter 1990) and *Predators and Prizes, American Privateering*, C. Swanson (Columbia S.C. 1991).

The Anglo-Dutch Wars of the Seventeenth Century, J. R. Jones (London 1996) assesses these complex conflicts in context, while *The Dutch Navy in the Seventeenth and Eighteenth Centuries*, J. R. Bruijn (Columbia S.C. 1993), *Cromwell's Navy*, B. Capp (Oxford 1989) and *Gentlemen and Tarpaulins; the Restoration Navy*, J. D. Davies (Oxford 1991) analyse the navies. *The Crisis of French Seapower, 1688–97: from guerre d'escadre to guerre de course*, G. Symcox (The Hague 1974) examines the failure of the French bid for naval mastery. *England and the War of the Spanish Succession, 1702–1712*, J. B. Hattendorf (New York 1987) examines the pivotal war in which England became the foremost seapower.

Louis XV's Navy (Quebec 1987) and *Anatomy of Naval Disaster* (Toronto 1996), both by J. Pritchard, provide a fresh insight into the flaws of the French Navy. *Amphibious warfare in the 18th century*, R. H. Harding (Woodbridge 1991) examines the 1739–43 campaign in the West Indies, but makes far wider reflections. *The Bells of Victory*, R. Middleton (Cambridge 1985) updates *England in the Seven Years War*, Julian Corbett's (London 1907) masterpiece. *Navies, Deterrence and American Independence, Britain and Seapower in the 1760s and 1770s*, N. Tracey (Vancouver 1988) examines the use of naval power as a diplomatic instrument. In *The War for America*, P. Mackesy (London 1964) provides the context for the complex and shifting campaigns of that conflict. *The Royal Navy in European Waters 1778–1783*, D. Syrett (Columbia S.C. 1998) offers a new study of the generally under-researched theatre.

Major studies of the naval campaigns of 1793–1815 are surprisingly rare. *Soldiers, Sugar and Seapower: The British Expeditions to the West Indies and the War against Revolutionary France*, M. Duffy (Oxford 1987), *The War in the Mediterranean, 1803–1810*, Mackesy (London 1957) and *The Campaign of Trafalgar*, Julian Corbett (London 1910) are among the best.

Trafalgar and the Spanish Navy, J. Harbron (London 1989) covers the entire century. Among biographies of Nelson, which are far too numerous, those by A. T. Mahan (1897), C. Oman (1947) and T. Pocock (1987) are the most useful. For the wider context see *Nelson's Navy*, B. Lavery (London 1989).

For the United States Navy and the War of 1812, *A Gentlemanly and Honourable Profession: the creation of the US Naval officer corps, 1787–1815*, C. McKee (Annapolis 1991) is invaluable; *Navalists and Anti-Navalists, the naval policy debate in the United States, 1785–1827*, C. L. Symonds (Newark 1980) widens the discussion. *Stoddert's war; the Quasi-war with France 1798–1801*, M. A. Palmer (Columbia S.C. 1987) covers the first service of the new force. *The War of 1812: A Forgotten Conflict*, D. R. Hickey (Urbana Ill. 1989), *Mr Madison's War: Politics, Diplomacy and Warfare in the early American Republic 1783–1830*, J. C. A. Stagg (Princeton 1983) and *The War of 1812: Land Operations*, G. F. G. Stanley (Ottawa 1983) offer the best overall coverage of strategy, politics and combat, while *The Battle of Lundy's Lane: On the Niagara in 1814*, D. E. Graves (Baltimore 1993) is among the finest studies of a battle yet written. *Cockburn and the British Navy in Transition: Admiral Sir George Cockburn 1772–1853*, R. Morriss (Exeter 1997) and *Broke and the Shannon*, P. Padfield (London 1968) assess the two British naval heroes of the war.

For the post-1815 Royal Navy, see *Great Britain and Seapower 1815–1853*, C. J. Bartlett (Oxford 1963) and *The Last Sailing Battlefleet: Maintaining Naval mastery 1815–1850*, A. D. Lambert (London 1991). *Russian Seapower and the Eastern Question, 1827–1841*, J. C. K. Daly (London 1991) asks fundamental questions about Russian naval power.

The range of material available of the naval wars of this period is simply astonishing. Original manuscripts have been widely published, notably by the British Navy Records Society (founded 1893, over 140 volumes published), the United States Naval Historical Center, and (earlier works) the French government. The collected correspondence of Nelson, John Paul Jones, and other famous admirals, and the memoirs of less famous seamen add a personal touch.

Index

Figures in *italic* refer to captions

Abercromby, General, *170–71*
Aboukir Bay, *162–3*, 163–6, *170–71*
Ache, Admiral d', 121
Achille, *159*, 184
Acre, 167, *214*, 215
Admiralty (Britain), 89, 111
Aix-la-Chapelle, Treaty of (1748), 114
Albemarle, George Monck, Duke of 61, 63, 67, 69, *70*, 71
Albermarle, General the Earl of, 125
Alcide, *126–7*
Alexandria, 161, 163
Algiers, 194, 211, 212
Amiens, Peace of (1802), 170, 174
amphibious warfare, 31–2, 99
Amphion, *94–5*
Amsterdam, 186
anchors, *31*
Anglo-Dutch wars, 36, 56–7, *57–77*, *62*, *64–5*, *70–73*, *76*
Anson, Commodore George, 111, 112–13, 117, 118, 119, 120, 124–5, 134, 135, 137, 220
Anson's Bay, *208–9*
Antwerp, 81, 186, 189–90, 191
arms races, 27
Association, 92, *92–3*
Atlantic Ocean, 113, 197
Augustus II, king of Saxony, 96
Austria, 154, 166, 167, 177

Bainbridge, William, 197
Baltic:
    amphibious warfare, 31–2
    in the eighteenth century, 95–103
    Great Northern War, 96–9, *97*, *99*
    Russian fleet, 210
    trade with Dutch, 58, 60

Baltimore, 204, *205*
Bank of England, 88–9
Bantry Bay, battle of (1689), 83
Barfleur, *128–9*
Barfleur, Cape, 85
Barham, Admiral Lord, 176
Bart, Jean, 89, 220
battleships, 35, 36–8, *38–9*, *213*, *216–17*
Baudin, Admiral, *212*, 213
Beachy Head, battle of (1690), 83–4, *84–5*, 88
Belgium, 114, 154, 170–71, 174, 191, *212–13*
Belle-Île, 121, *124*, 127
Bellerophon, 165, 191
Berkeley, Admiral, 69–71
Black Sea, *32–3*, 101, *101*, 102, 103, 210
Blake, Robert, 60, 61, 63, 67, 220
Blane, Sir Gilbert, 142
Bligh, Captain William, 49, *54–5*
blockades, 23–5, *24–5*, 39
Bombay, 67, 121
Bonhomme Richard, 138
Boscawen, Admiral, 116, 119
Boston, 197, *200–201*
Boston Tea Party (1773), 132
Boulogne, 170, 174
Bounty, 49, 55
Bourbon dynasty, 107, 124, 130–31, 149, 152
Boyne, battle of the (1689), 83
Brazil, 188, 197
Breda, Peace of (1667), 73
Brederode, 59
Brest, *28–9*, 44, 83, 85, 86, *117*, 118–19, 120, 121, 155, 156, 157, 160, 161, 174–5, 176–7, 185, 188
Breton, Cape, *113*
Bridport, Lord, 160

Britain:
  Anglo-Dutch wars, 36, 56–7,
    57–77, 62, 64–5, 70–73, 76
  Anglo-Spanish wars, 67, 111
  battleships, 35, 38, 38–9
  French Revolutionary wars, 39,
    150–51, 155–71, 156, 158–9,
    164–6
  global power, 106, 107, 114, 131
  Great Northern War, 98
  Greek War of Independence,
    211–12
  growth of navy, 106, 114–15
  guns, 45–8, 131
  merchant ships, 35, 60
  mutinies, 54, 161
  Napoleonic Wars, 39, 173–91,
    178, 180–83, 188–9
  naval bases, 44–5, 110
  nineteenth-century naval warfare,
    210–17
  seamen, 51, 52, 54–5, 76–7
  Seven Years War, 116–27, 122–4,
    126–7
  shipbuilding, 36, 42, 44, 131, 187
  tactics, 48–9, 66
  War of American Independence,
    46–7, 49, 128–9, 131–49,
    139–45, 154
  War of the Austrian Succession,
    111–14
  War of Jenkins's Ear, 107–10
  War of 1812, 193–206, 194–5,
    200–201, 205–7
  War of the Spanish Succession, 90,
    106
  wars with France, 80, 83–90, 84–5
Britannia, 86
Brock, General Isaac, 196
Broke, Sir Philip, 18, 47, 197–203,
  201
Brueys, Admiral, 164
Brunswick, 157–9, 159
Bucentaure, 182, 183, 184, 185

Buenos Aires, 131, 186
Burgoyne, General John, 133
Byng, Admiral Sir George, 106
Byng, Admiral Sir John, 117–18

Cádiz, 24–5, 119, 160, 175, 176–7,
  184
Calais, 89
Calder, Admiral Sir Robert, 176,
  177
Camperdown, battle of (1797), 161
Canada, 112, 113, 116, 118, 119,
  122–3, 127, 133, 196, 197, 203–4,
  206
Canning, George, 211
cannon, 45–6
Cape of Good Hope, 160, 186
Cape St Vincent, 213
  battle of (1693), 88
  battle of (1780), 138, 139
  battle of (1797), 160
Caribbean, 23, 110, 194
Carron Company, 46
carronades, 46, 131
Cartagena, 110, 175
Centurion, 111
Ceylon, 149, 160, 191
Champlain, Lake, 133, 194, 204
Charles I, king of England, 41, 66
Charles II, king of England, 67, 68,
  69, 73–4, 75, 76
Charles III, king of Spain, 124
Charles X, king of France, 212
Charles XII, king of Sweden, 96–9
Chatham, 73, 73
Cherbourg, 86, 119, 152–4
Chesapeake, USS, 196, 197–202,
  200–201
Chesapeake Bay, 140–41, 197, 204
Chesmé, battle of (1770), 101, 101
La Chevrette, 150–51
China, 37, 208–9, 215
Choiseul, Duc de, 130, 131, 133
Clive, Robert, 121

Cochrane, Admiral Sir Alexander, 204
Cochrane, Lord, 37, *188–9*, 189, 211, 220–21
Cockburn, Admiral Sir George, 191, *192–3*, 197, 204, 205, 221
Codrington, Sir Edward, 184, 211–12
Colbert, Jean-Baptiste, 80–81, 82, 93, 130, 221
Collingwood, Admiral Cuthbert, *41*, 160, 177, 178–81, *180*, 184
Conflans, Admiral, 120
Congreve, William, 174
Constitution, USS, 197
Cook, Captain James, 51, 119, 131, *132*
Copenhagen, 167–8, *168–9*, 187–8, *187*
Corbett, Sir Julian, 23
Cordoba, Admiral de, 160
Cornwallis, Admiral Sir William, 138, 145, 160, 174–6, 177, 191
Cromwell, Oliver, 66, 67, 73
Cuba, 107, 124–5, *126–7*

de la Clue, 119
Deane, General-at-Sea, 63
Decatur, Captain Stephen, 197, 205, *207*, 221
Den Helder, 161, 186
Denmark, 26, 44, 96, 98, 100, 167–8, *168–9*, 187–8, *187*
Deptford, *36*, 52
Diadem, 142
dockyards, *28–9*, 30, *36*, 44–5
Dogger Bank, battle of (1781), 146
Dominica, 121, 139
Downs, battle of the (1639), 59
Drake, Sir Francis, 111
dry docks, *36*, 42, 44
Duguay-Trouin, René, 93, 222
Duke, *47*
Dumanoir, Admiral, 184

Duncan, Admiral Lord, 161
Dunkirk, 80–81, 89, 156
Duperre, Admiral, 212

East India Company (English), 67, 126, *208–9*
East Indies, *26*, 58, 60, 67, 146, 148, 190
Eendracht, 69
Egypt, 161–6, 167, *170–71*, 211–12, *214*, 215
El Morro, siege of (1762), 125, *126–7*
Endymion, *207*
England *see* Britain
English Channel, *26*, 60, 61–3, 66, 81, 112–13, 146, 174–5, 216–17
Erie, Lake, 197, 203
Essex, HMS, 120
Etats de Bourgogne, 130
Evertsen, Admiral Cornelis, 71
Excellent, 55
Exmouth, Admiral Lord, 211

Farmer, Captain, *117*
Ferdinand VI, king of Spain, 124
Ferrol, 175, 176
Finisterre, Cape, 113, 176, 184
Finland, 102
Finland, Gulf of, 98, 102
fireships, 36–7, *37*, 101
Fisher, Admiral John, 191
fisheries, 60
Flamborough Head, 138
Florida, 127, 130, 134, 149
Flushing, 186, 190
Foley, Captain, 164–5, *165*
Forbin, Chevalier, 93
Formidable, 141–2
Four Days battle (1666), 56–7, 69–71, *70*–72, 76
France:
    Algerian war, 212
    and Anglo-Dutch Wars, 58, 69, 74, 75, 76

battleships, 35, 38, *213*
Caribbean 'Quasi-War', 194
dockyards, *28–9*, 44
frigates, 107, 114–15
guerre de course, 31, 89
guns, 45, 47–8, 115–16
increases size of navy, 152–4
Napoleonic Wars, 173–91, *178*,
  180–83, *188–9*
Revolutionary wars, 51, 55,
  150–51, 154–67, *156*, *158–9*,
  164–6, 170–71, *170–71*
rise and fall of navy, 79–93, 107,
  114–15
seamen, 51, 52
Seven Years War, 116–24, *122–4*,
  126–7, 130
shipbuilding, 42, 44, 81, 186–7
tactics, 48–9
War of American Independence,
  46–7, 49, *128–9*, 134–7, 138–46,
  140–45, 148–9
War of the Austrian Succession,
  111–14
War of the Spanish Succession,
  90
Frederick II, king of Prussia, 118
Frederickshamn, battle of (1790),
  94–5
frigates, 35, *59*, 107, 114–15
Fulton, Robert, 174

Gabbard Shoal, battle of (1653), 63,
  64–5
galleys, *20–21*, 37
Gambier, Admiral, *189*
Ganteaume, Admiral, 175, 176, 177
Genoa, 186, 191
George I, king of England, 98
George II, king of England, 111
Gibraltar, *33*, 90, 93, 118, 119, 134,
  137, 138, 139, *139*, 146–7, *148*,
  149, 163, 176
Glorieux, 142

Glorious First of June, battle of
  (1794), 29, *158–9*, 159, 191
Goliath, 164, *164–5*
Gouden Leeuw, 76
Grasse, Admiral François-Joseph
  Paul de, *47*, *128–9*, 138–41, 142,
  143, 221–2
Graves, Admiral, 139, *141*, 146
Gravina, Admiral, 177
Great Fire of London (1666), 73
Great Lakes, 196–7, 203
Great Northern War (1700–21),
  96–100, *97*, 99
Greek War of Independence
  (1822–7), 211–12
Greenwich Naval Hospital, *86–7*,
  87
Grenada, 138
Grotius, Hugo, *58*
Guadeloupe, 121, 190
guerre de course, 31, 89
Guerrier, 164
Guerriere, HMS, 197
Guichen, Admiral de, 138, 146
guns, 33, 39, 45–8, 115–16, 131, 213
Gustavus III, king of Sweden, *94–5*,
  102

Hamilton, Lady, *166*
Hango Head, battle of (1714), 98,
  99
Hanover, 118, 119
Hanoverian dynasty, 106, 111
Hardwicke, Lord Chancellor, 111
Hardy, Admiral Sir Charles, 137, 146
Harrison, John, *93*
Havana, 124–5, *126–7*, 127
Hawke, Edward, 112, 113, 120–21
Henry VIII, king of England, 45
Hermione, 54
Hoche, General, 160
Hodgson, Colonel, *124*
Holland, 74, 114, 170–71, 174
  see also Netherlands

Holmes, Admiral, 72
Hood, Samuel, Viscount, *128–9*, *135*, 139, 141, 142–5, *144*, 145, 154, *156*, 157, 160, 166, 222
Hoste, Captain Sir William, 191
Hotham, Admiral, 160
Howe, Richard, Earl, 119, 120, 133, 134, 146–7, *148*, 149, 156–9, *159*, 161, 166, 223
Howe, General Sir William, 133, 134
Hudson River, 119, 133
Hughes, Admiral Sir Edward, 148
Hull, Isaac, 197
Hull, General William, 196

Imperieuse, 188–9
impressment, 26, 50, 77
India, 112, 113, 121, 148
Indian Ocean, 36, 190
Inscription Maritime, 50
Ireland, 83, 160, 161

Jackson, Andrew, 205
Jacobin, 157
Jacobins, 155, 157
Jamaica, *47*, 67, 110, 139, 145
James II, king of England, 68, 69, 74, *75*, 83, 85, 86–7
Java, 197
Jefferson, Thomas, 196
Jenkins, Captain Robert, 107–10
Jones, John Paul, 102, 138, 223–4

Kempenfelt, Richard, 137, 146, 147
Keppel, Admiral Sir Augustus, *124*, 125, 134–7
Key, Francis Scott, 204, *205*

La Galissonière, Admiral de, 117, 118
La Hougue, battle of (1692), 78–9, 86–7, *86*
Lagos, 119–20, 125

Langara, Admiral, 138
Lawrence, Captain James, 197–9, *201*, 202
Le Havre, 120, 156
League of Augsburg, war of (1688–97), 82–3
Leopard, 196
Lestock, Admiral, 112
line of battle, 48–9, 66, 77
Lisbon, 160, 188, 190
Lissa, battle of (1811), 191
Little Belt, 196
littoral warfare, 100, 103
London, 73, 119
London, 74
longitude, 92
Louis, Admiral, 177
Louis XIV, king of France, 73–4, 79, 80–81, 82–3, 85
Louis XV, king of France, 115, 130, 131
Louis XVI, king of France, 133
Louisbourg, 112, *113*, 114, 118, 119
Lowestoft, battle of (1665), 68–9
Lucas, Captain, 183
Lundy's Lane, battle of (1814), 203

Macdonough, Commodore Thomas, 204
Macedonian, 197
Madison, James, 196, 204, 206
Madras, 112, 114, 121
Magnanime, 120
Malaga, 90
Malta, *33*, 163, 167, 174, 191
Manila, 111, 126, 127, 131
Martinique, 121, 138, 190
Mary II, Queen of England, 83, *86*, 87
Matthews, Admiral, 112
Mauritius, 156, 190, 191
Mediterranean, *32–3*, 58, 89
  British control of, 93
  French fleet, 80

French Revolutionary wars, 156,
  160, 161–2, 166
Napoleonic Wars, 175
pirates, 60, 67
Russo-Turkish wars, 101
Seven Years War, 117–18, 119
War of the Spanish Succession, 90
Medway, battle of the (1667), *73*
Mehmet Ali, Pasha, 215
merchant ships, 31, 35–6, 39, 60
Mexico, 213, 216
Minorca, *33*, 93, 111, 117–18, *124*,
  134, 137, 146, 149
Monroe Doctrine, 211
Montagne, 157
Montevideo, 186
mutinies, 54, 161

Nantes, Edict of, 82
Napier, Sir Charles, 213, 215, 216,
  224
Naples, 155, 166, *166*, 167, 186
Napoleon I, Emperor, 23, 161–3,
  163, 167, 170, 174, 176, 177, 179,
  185–91, 196
Napoleonic wars (1803–15), 39, 51,
  152, 173–91, *178*, *180–83*, *188–9*
Narva, battle of (1700), 96, 98
naval bases, 44–5, 110
naval organization, 29–55
Navarino Bay, battle of (1827),
  211–12
navigation, 92
Navigation Acts, 60, 66, 77
Nelson, Admiral Lord, *117*, *135*,
  145, 170, *172–3*, 175, 191, 224
  battle of Copenhagen, 167–8,
    168–9
  battle of Trafalgar, 49, 176–85,
    178, *180–83*
  blockade of Cadiz, *24–5*
  death, *6*, 183, 184, 185
  French Revolutionary wars,
    160–61
  injuries, 160, 161, 165, 203
  in Naples, *166*, 167
  Nile campaign, 163–7, *164–5*
  subordination of prize to glory,
    51
Nemesis, *208–9*
Neptune, 178
Netherlands:
  Anglo-Dutch wars, 36, 56–7,
    57–77, *62*, *64–5*, *70–73*, 76
  East Indies trade, *26*
  French Revolutionary wars, 160,
    161
  Great Northern War, 98
  Napoleonic Wars, 191
  shipbuilding, 42
  tactics, 48, 58–9
  Treaty of Aix-la-Chapelle, 114
  War of American Independence,
    146, 148
  War of the Spanish Succession,
    90
  wars with France, 80–82, 83, *84–5*
New England, 197, 206
New Orleans, *194*, 205
New York, 68, 75, 132–3, 134, 197,
  204, 205
Newcastle, Duke of, 118
Newfoundland, 60, 75, 93, 149
Nile, battle of (1798), 164–7,
  164–5, *178*, 191
Nootka Sound, 154
Nore, 161
Normandy, 86, 119
North Africa, 23, 67, 211
North America, 112
  British colonies, 67
  Seven Years War, 116, *122–4*, 125,
    127
  War of American Independence,
    128–9, 131–4, 138–9, *140–41*,
    149, 194
North Sea, 58, 60, 66
Northumberland, 191

Nymegen, Treaty of (1678), 82
Nystad, Peace of (1721), 99

oared ships, 37
Ochakov, 101–2, 154
officers, 51, 54, 55, 76–7
Ontario, Lake, 119, 197, 203
Opdam, Admiral, 68–9
L'Orient, 163, 165
Orion, 184
Orvilliers, Admiral d', 134–6

Pacific Ocean, 111, 131
Paixhans, General Henri, 48, 213
Pakenham, Sir Edward, 205
Palliser, Admiral Sir Hugh, 135,
    136, 137
Palmerston, Lord, 212–13, 215, 216
Paris, Peace of (1763), 127
Parker, Admiral Sir Hyde, 167–8
Parker, Admiral Sir William, 191,
    215, 216
Paul, Tsar, 167, 168
Pearson, Captain Richard, 138
Peninsular War (1808–14), 190
Pepys, Samuel, 224–5
Perry, Commodore Oliver Hazard,
    203
Peter the Great, Tsar, 98, 100
Philip II, king of Spain, 110
Philip V, king of Spain, 106
Pigot, Captain Hugh, 54
pirates, 23, 67, 211
Pitt, William the Elder, 118, 121,
    122, 124, 124
Pitt, William the Younger, 154, 156
Plymouth, 52, 89, 120, 121, 131,
    137
Pocock, Admiral Sir George, 121,
    125
Poland, 42, 96
Poltava, battle of (1709), 98
Portland, battle of (1653), 63
Portsmouth, 52, 131, 137, 147

Portugal, 67, 106, 119–20, 127, 166,
    188, 190, 213
President, HMS, 206–7
President, USS, 196, 205, 207
Prevost, General, 204, 205
Prince, 76
privateers, 23, 31, 36, 67, 88, 89, 93,
    113, 138
Prussia, 118, 155, 185, 186

Quebec, 106, 119, 133
Quebec, HMS, 117
Queen Charlotte, 157
Quiberon Bay, battle of (1759),
    104–5, 120–21, 122–3, 125

Redoutable, 182–3, 185
Resolution, 120
Restoration, 67
Revolutionary Wars, 39, 52–3, 130
Rochefort, 81, 120, 175, 176, 177, 188
Rodney, Admiral Sir George, 47,
    120, 138–42, 139, 143, 179, 225
Rooke, Admiral Sir George, 86, 90,
    91, 225
Ross, General Sir Robert, 204
Royal Charles, 69, 73, 74
Royal George, 120, 147, 147
Royal James, 74–5
Royal Navy see Britain
Royal Prince, 71, 71, 74
Royal Sovereign, 41, 72, 76
Royal Sovereign II, 40–41
Royal Sovereign III, 40–41, 40, 160,
    178–9, 181
Royal Sovereign IV, 40–41, 216–17,
    217
Rupert, Prince, 69, 70, 71–2, 75, 76
Russell, Admiral Sir Edward, 85–6,
    88–9
Russia, 23, 154
    Great Northern war, 96–100, 99
    Napoleonic wars, 166, 167, 168,
        177, 185, 187, 190, 196

Russo-Turkish wars, 36, 100–102, *101*
war with Sweden, 102–3
Ruyter, Michiel Adrianszoon de, *57*, 63, 69, 71, 72, 73, 74–5, 77, 82, 222
Ryswick, Peace of (1697), 89

Sackett's Harbour, 203
sailors, 49–55
sails, *34–5*
St André, Jeanbon, 155, 157
St Lawrence, 203
St Lawrence River, 119, 203
St Malo, 89, 119
St Michael, 74
St Petersburg, 98, 102
St Vincent, John Jervis, Earl, 119, 160, 161, 163, 167, 174–5, 191, 223
Saintes, battle of the (1782), *46–7*, 49, *128–9*, 141–5, *142–5*
San Josef, 160
San Nicolas, 160
Sandwich, Lord, 69, 74–5
Santa Anna, 181
Santa Cruz, battle of (1657), 67
Santander, 190
Santissima Trinidad, 152, *153*, 183–4
Saratoga, 133–4
Saumarez, James de, 145
Saunders, Admiral, 119
Saxe, Marshal de, 114
Scheldt, River, 81, 154, 190
Scheveningen, battle of (1653), 63, 66
Schooneveld, second battle of the (1673), 75
Scilly Isles, 92, *92–3*, 146
Scotland, 63, 112, 119, 120
Scott, General Winfield, 203, 216
scurvy, 52, 110, 121, 131
seamen, 49–55

seapower, 22–6
Second Coalition, 166, 167
Seignelay, Marquis de, 82
Selden, John, 58
Senegal, 121, 127, 149
Serapis, 138
Seven Years War (1756–63), 52, 55, 116–27, *122–4*, *126–7*, 130
Shannon, 18, 47, 197–202, *200–201*
ships, 33–8
    battleships, 35, 36–8, *38–9*, *213*, *216–17*
    cruisers, 36
    fireships, 36–7, *37*, 101
    frigates, 35, 59, 107, 114–15
    galleys, *20–21*, 37
    guns, 33, 39, 45–8, 115–16, 131, 213
    life at sea, 49–55
    merchant ships, 35–6, 39
    rigs, 33, *34*, 37
    sails, *34–5*
    shipbuilding, 38–45, *43*, 131, 186–7
    steam power, 215–16, *216–17*, 217
    tactics, 48–9
'ships of the line', 33–5
Shovell, Sir Cloudesley, 90–93, *90*, *92–3*
Sicily, 106, 167, 177
Sinavin, Admiral, 188
Smith, Captain Sir Sidney, 167
Smyrna convoy, 88
soldiers, 51
Sole Bay, battle of (1672), 74
Le Soleil Royale, *78–9*, 85–6, 120
Sovereign of the Seas, 40–41, 61
Spain, 60
    Anglo-Spanish wars, 67, 111
    battle of Cape Passaro, 106
    French Revolutionary wars, 160
    increases size of navy, 152–4, *153*
    Napoleonic Wars, 49, 174, 176, 190

Seven Years War, 125, *126–7*, 130
War of American Independence, 134, 137, *139*, 146–9
War of Jenkins's Ear, 107–10
War of the Spanish Succession, 90
wars with France, 81–2, 90
Spithead, 147, *147*, 156, 161
Spragge, Admiral, *76*
steam power, 215–16, *216–17*, 217
Stuart, Charles Edward, 112
Stuart dynasty, 88, 89, 112
Suffren, Pierre André de, 148, 225
Surcouf, Robert, 226
Surveillante, *117*
Svensksund, battle of (1790), *95*, 102–3
Sweden:
  dry docks, 44
  Great Northern War, 96–100, *97*, *99*
  guns, 45
  war with Russia, 102–3
Syria, 167, 215

tactics, 48–9
taxation, 23, 26, 30
Temeraire, 178, 183
Texel, battle of the (1673), *75*, 76
Thames, battle of (1813), 203
Thames estuary, 68, 69
Thesée, *104–5*
Theseus, *24–5*
Tilsit, Treaty of (1807), 185, 187
Tobago, 138, 149
Torbay, 120, 121
Torrington, Arthur Herbert, Earl of, 83–4, 85, 137
Toulon, 44, 69, 155, 156, *156*, 157, 163, 166, 175
Toulon, battle of (1744), 112, 137
Toulouse, Comte de, 90
Tourville, Anne-Hilarion de Cotentin, Comte de, 83–6, 88, 137, 226

Trafalgar, battle of (1805), 23, *41*, 49, 178–85, *178*, *180–83*, 191, 202
Tromp, Cornelis, *76*
Tromp, Admiral Maerten Harpertszoon, 59, 60, 61–3, 226
Troubridge, Captain Thomas, 160, 164, *166*, 167
Turkey, 36, 100–102, *101*, 166, 188, 211–12, 215

Ukraine, 98, 102
United States, USS, 197
United States of America:
  dry docks, 44
  Mexican War, 216
  Monroe Doctrine, 211
  nineteenth-century navy, 138, 202, 210–11
  shipbuilding, 39, 44
  War of 1812, 51, 193–206, *194–5*, *200–201*, *205–7*
Ushakov, Admiral, 102
Ushant, battle of (1778), 135–7
Utrecht, Treaty of, 93

van Ghent, Admiral, 74
Vauban, Marshal, 88
Vengeur du Peuple, 157–9, *159*
Venice, 186, 191
Vera Cruz, *212*, 213, 216
Vergennes, Comte de, 133–4, 149, 152
Vernon, Admiral Edward, 110
Versailles, Peace of (1783), 149
Viborg, Bay of, 102, 103
Victory, 6, 135, *135*, 146, 147, *148*, 160, 178, 182–3, *182–3*, 184, 202
Vienna, Congress of (1814–15), 191
Vigo, 90, *91*, 176
Villaret-Joyeuse, Admiral, 157, 160
Ville de Paris, *128–9*, 130, 142
Villeneuve, Pierre Charles, 165, 175–8, 182, 184, 185, 226

Voltaire, François Marie Arouet de, 118

Walcheren, 75, 190
War of the Austrian Succession (1741–8), 111–14
War of Jenkins's Ear (1739), 107–10
War of 1812, 51, 193–206, *194–5, 200–201, 205–7*
War of the Spanish Succession (1702–14), 89–90, 106
Washington, DC, *191, 192–3,* 204, *205*
Washington, George, 132, 133
Watt, James, 46
Wellington, Duke of, 190, 197, 204
West Indies, 58, 67, 107–11, 113, 120, 121, 134, 135, 138, 139, 146, 155, 156, 175–6, 190
Western Approaches, 112–13, 134, 155
Western Squadron, 113, 118–19, 121, 135, 146
Westminster, Treaty of (1654), 66, 75–6
Westphalia, Treaty of (1648), 154
William III, king of England, 75, 82, 83, 89
Winter, Admiral de, 161
Witt, John de, 68, 75
Wolfe, James, 119
wood, shipbuilding, 39–44

Yorktown, battle of (1781), 138, 139, *140–41,* 149

Zealand, 61, 74, 187–8
Zeven Provincien, 57

Picture credits

Every effort has been made to contact the copyright holders for images reproduced in this book. The publishers would welcome any errors or omissions being brought to their attention.